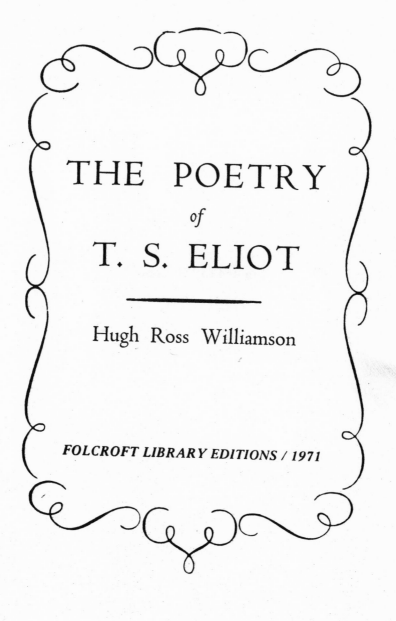

THE POETRY

of

T. S. ELIOT

Hugh Ross Williamson

FOLCROFT LIBRARY EDITIONS / 1971

Limited to 150 Copies

THE POETRY

of

T. S. ELIOT

Hugh Ross Williamson

LONDON
HODDER & STOUGHTON LIMITED
1932

PRINTED IN GREAT BRITAIN FOR HODDER AND STOUGHTON, LIMITED
BY RICHARD CLAY AND SONS, LIMITED, BUNGAY, SUFFOLK.

For
H. R. W. and G. W. W.

I should like to express my gratitude to Mr. Eliot for his kindness in supplying certain facts of which I have made use in this book, and for the stimulus of his conversation.

H. R. W.

Contents

I

Apology

ENTHUSIASM needs apology, since it transgresses the Unwritten Law of modern criticism, which allows only languid patronage or extravagant rhapsody. And while the first is perhaps only a natural caution inspired by the monotonous discovery of a masterpiece a week, the second must not be mistaken for enthusiasm. It is ennui. Rhapsody writers are merely people paid to supply testimonials. Their early interest in analysing the contents of the bottle before recommending it as a universal panacea has waned ; and without trial they certify it as " the mixture as before."

I cannot say that " Mr. Eliot has an aptitude for writing pleasant little verses," or that " Mr. Eliot is indubitably the greatest poet of all time," either of which would comply with

9

the requirements of critical jargon. My less
challenging or impertinent belief is that Mr.
T. S. Eliot is the most important influence in
English poetry at the present time ; that, more
than any other single man, he has helped to
change the course of it ; that his " The Waste
Land " of 1922 is comparable with Wordsworth's and Coleridge's " Lyrical Ballads " of
1798, both as a turning-point and as a force ;
and that English poetry of the future will be
largely unintelligible to those unacquainted with
his work. These considerations, themselves indicative of enthusiasm, are my justification for
attempting this commenting.

Especially the last. For this book is for the
Plain Reader, the lover of poetry who is puzzled
by Mr. Eliot's " difficulty " and bewildered
by the critical controversies which, in " high-
brow " circles, still occasionally rage round his
name. The fact that T. S. Eliot is an estab-
lished and even slightly out-moded institution
among writers in their twenties, and that by
them his importance has long been taken for

granted, does not, unfortunately, affect the complementary fact that to the vast majority of older readers he is either unknown or regarded with suspicion.

This unpopularity is due to several causes. In the first place, he is an aristocratic poet writing in a democratic age, a Classicist among the lees of Romanticism. Enjoyment of his poetry depends partly on knowledge of past poets ; at the least, it presupposes a humanist culture. This is a serious drawback in an epoch which has invented " vocational training " and encouraged new universities as utilitarian adjuncts to Big Business.

In the second place, most of the key positions in criticism are occupied by people who have, as it were, a vested interest in denying Mr. Eliot a hearing. Criticism of poetry is mainly entrusted to the elder poets. It is in the hands of the " Georgians," to whom Mr. Eliot is very properly anathema, because once his conception of poetry is understood and his work appreciated, most of the " Georgians " will be dismissed for ever as the negligible versifiers that they are.

In the third place, Mr. Eliot is not an " escapist." Poetry is now popularly regarded as a drug. It is not even an intelligent pastime. The crossword-puzzle enthusiast would be hurt and resentful if it were suggested that he should bring to the reading of poetry one-twentieth part of the mental effort which he devotes daily to his chosen sport. " Poetry " is just something that enables him to pack up his troubles in his old kit-bag and take an excursion to the lake isle of Innisfree. But Mr. Eliot refuses to allow his reader to escape. He insists that he remain where he is and *think* ; that he transform what is ugly in his environment, and, if that is impossible, that he honestly recognise its ugliness, instead of crying " beauty " where there is no beauty.

In the fourth place, Mr. Eliot is too cosmopolitan. His masters are the French Symbolists (he even writes poems in French), his passion is Dante, and even among the great English poets he prefers the later Shakespeare, the lesser known Elizabethans, Donne and the Metaphysicals, Dryden and the Classicists. He seldom, if ever, mentions Alfred, Lord Tennyson. This " popular " deficiency in him may be illustrated by quoting Sir Henry Newbolt's excellent tribute to the present Poet Laureate : " It is not only by his love of ships, of horses, of sport, and of poetry that Masefield is so typically English : his method in writing, whether narrative, dramatic, lyrical or reflective, shows the ready-and-willing practical character of the Englishman. His impulse seems to be always free, never for a moment hampered by theory or anxiety. He is the good, though not the highly skilled, workman who will undertake to use any material in any familiar style." This, with the exception of the love of poetry, describes practically everything that T. S. Eliot is not. He has composed no poems about sport or ships or horses. His writing, far from reflecting a ready-and-willing impulse, is highly formal and reluctant to divulge its secrets. He

is an extraordinarily highly-skilled workman
who has spent years in discovering and perfect-
ing an individual technique, and even when he
adopts a familiar style he is fastidious in his
choice of material.

Yet, in spite of these handicaps, it is necessary for him to be understood—necessary, that
is, if English poetry is to continue to be read
outside a small clique. For, though he is still
unknown to many readers, he is a dominating
influence on writers, and has been for the last
five years. It is no exaggeration to say that
there is no young poet at present writing who
does not owe something to T. S. Eliot. The
verse of the new generation will conform to his
vision (this does not mean that it will be imi-
tative or derivative) ; and, when the youngest
" Georgian " is at last extinct, and the supply
of conventional romantic poetry comes to an
end, there will be nothing contemporary for the
non-Eliotite to read.

It is necessary, too, for another reason. Until
Mr. Eliot's method is studied, it is impossible

to see the work of other poets in right relation
to his.   The Plain Reader, misled by the critics
and glancing superficially at some of Mr. Eliot's
poems, might be inclined to connect him with,
for instance, Miss Edith Sitwell.   No classifica-
tion could be more untrue.   Apart altogether
from their relative values as poets, Miss Sitwell
is Romantic and anarchic while Mr. Eliot is
Classical and traditional.

   It is possible to take four lines of " The
Waste Land " out of their context :

> " Twit twit twit
> Jug jug jug jug jug jug
> So rudely forc'd
> Tereu,"

and indulge in the easy sneer that this is not
classicism, but chaos.   Isolated from its context, of course it is.   But it cannot be so
isolated, any more than the poem itself can be
judged by Romantic canons.   Yet it occasionally
happens that inferior writers, not comprehend-
ing the spirit, have adopted the style to express
their own unimportant emotions, relying on
obscurity to cover their lack of thought.   They

succeed in imposing themselves on readers as
" modernists," only because the readers have
not the requisite knowledge of the genuine
article to recognise the bogus imitation.

Above all, it is necessary to understand Mr.
Eliot so that he may himself be criticised. It
is pointless to find fault with an eagle because
it does not act like a dove. Most of the criticism directed against Mr. Eliot is valueless for
this reason. Comprehension must precede criticism. So this book is only a commentary ; its
aim, elucidation. I have tried as far as possible
to suppress my own views in order to present
his with as little distortion as is humanly
possible. Though there are things in his attitude with which I profoundly disagree, I have
endeavoured not to obtrude my own prejudices.
If this book introduces the reader to his work,
it will have accomplished its purpose. The
battle can follow later. But the combatants
must know what they are fighting about.

Nor does disagreement in any way lessen my
enthusiasm.

II

The Man Behind the Poetry

[ELIOT, Thomas Stearns, M.A.; Editor, The Criterion; Director, Faber and Faber, Ltd.; *b.* 1888; *y.s.* of Henry Ware Eliot and Charlotte Chauncey Eliot of St. Louis, U.S.A.; *m.* Vivien, *d.* of Charles Haigh Haigh-Wood, London. *Educ.* Harvard University; the Sorbonne; Merton College, Oxford. *Publications :* The Sacred Wood, 1920; The Waste Land, 1922; Homage to John Dryden, 1924; Poems 1909–1925, 1925; An Essay in Poetic Drama, 1928; Shakespeare and the Stoicism of Seneca, 1928; For Lancelot Andrewes, 1928; Dante, 1929; Ash Wednesday, 1930; Thoughts after Lambeth, 1931. *Club :* Royal Societies.

TO this entry, reproduced by permission from " Who's Who, 1932," may be added the fact that T. S. Eliot is Charles Eliot Norton, Professor of Poetry, Harvard University, 1932–33.

These things constitute everything about the man behind the poetry that it is necessary to know or mannerly to inquire.

III

Exeunt the Romantics

TO compare one poet with another, which
often means to exalt the one at the expense
of the other, is, in general, the worst form of
criticism. Yet, in this case it is, I think, per-
missible to consider T. S. Eliot's work in relation to the background against which it appeared.
The position is peculiar. A certain type of
poetry was (and is) generally accepted and
popularly approved ; any verse not conforming
to its standards was (and is) condemned as
"not true poetry." As my chief aim is to
introduce Eliot's poetry to the reader who
already enjoys the Georgians, the obvious approach seems by way of them. By this means,
the divergence between Eliot and his elders will
be most easily understood.

John Drinkwater's "A Prayer" shows the

Georgians at their best ; he himself is their
most typical representative, and " A Prayer,"
besides being deservedly well known, is a genuine
attempt to express an emotional problem of
universal application—the failure of will.

" Lord, not for light in darkness do we pray,
   Not that the veil be lifted from our eyes,
   Nor that the slow ascension of our day
      Be otherwise.

    .   .   .   .   .

   We do not crave the high perception swift,
   When to refrain were well, and when fulfil,
   Nor yet the understanding strong to sift
      The good from ill.

   Not these, O Lord.   For these Thou hast reveal'd,
   We know the golden season when to reap
   The heavy-fruited treasure of the field,
      The hour to sleep.

   Not these. We know the hemlock from the rose,
   The pure from stain'd, the noble from the base,
   The tranquil holy light of truth that glows
      On Pity's face.

   We know the paths wherein our feet should press,
   Across our hearts are written Thy decrees :
   Yet now, O Lord, be merciful to bless
      With more than these.

Grant us the will to fashion as we feel,
Grant us the strength to labour as we know,
Grant us the purpose, ribb'd and edged with steel,
    To strike the blow.

Knowledge we ask not—knowledge Thou hast lent,
But, Lord, the will—there lies our bitter need,
Give us to build above the deep intent
    The deed, the deed."

These seven stanzas may be compared with twelve short lines from the closing section of Eliot's " The Hollow Men " :

" Between the idea
And the reality
Between the motion
And the act
Falls the Shadow
        For Thine is the Kingdom

Between the conception
And the creation
Between the emotion
And the response
Falls the Shadow
        Life is very long "

though it is perhaps unfair to take these two stanzas from their context, because thus they are robbed of much of their significance.

Examining the two extracts, we find that the regular soft beat of Drinkwater's padded lines produces the unctuous effect of a church organ, an atmosphere wherein emotions may dissolve into a comfortable vagueness. In spite of the theme, there is a sentimental self-pity about the expression of it. Confession becomes almost a pleasure. At the end, certainly, we experience a sense of " uplift," something of the spurious *Katharsis* which comes from singing a hearty hymn.

But Eliot is ruthless. There is no comfort in his poem. We are not sitting at ease in a pew, awaiting further titillation of our jaded emotional palates. We are penitents, bare knees on the stone, receiving words like lashes. We cannot even claim the consolation of thanking God for the things we know. For what do we know ?

> " Between the idea
> And the reality . . ."

In those two lines is incidentally concentrated the major part of philosophy for us to ponder.

And after two minutes' *thought* on that subject
of ideas and realities, which has baffled the
Ancients, the Mediævals and the Moderns, we
may possibly come to the conclusion that two
other lines :

> " The tranquil holy light of truth that glows
>   On Pity's face,"

mean less than we thought they did.

Here, then, are apparent two characteristics
of Eliot's work—the use of words which *mean*
something and the corresponding necessity of
thought on the reader's part. " Idea,"
" reality," " motion," " act," " conception,"
" creation," " emotion," " response," would
be as startlingly out of place in the inconse-
quential haze of " A Prayer " as would " the
heavy-fruited treasure of the field " in " The
Hollow Men." But, then, most of the Georgians are afflicted by what Eliot describes as " an
impotence to use words definitely, to use words
at all unless they are the few poor counters of
habitual and lazy sentiment."

Not only is he laboriously careful in his choice

of words, but he constantly uses quotations to evoke vast associations. The simple " For Thine is the Kingdom," with its immediate ascription of Almighty Power and its secondary reminder of the Perfect Prayer, implies also a definition of God, which is altogether lacking in the other poem. In addition, it provides a violent contrast between the impotence of man, dogged by the Shadow, and the power of God —a contrast in no way comparable with the feeble

" Knowledge we ask not—knowledge Thou hast lent,
But, Lord, the will—there lies our bitter need."

The difference between the scope of these two contrasts suggests another difference between the two approaches. Drinkwater is subjective, Eliot objective. The " Prayer " is personal ; " The Hollow Men " universal. But this does not mean that the former is more intense. Actually the reverse is true. In the universal the individual is included and the personal weakness heightened to the level of a general tragedy.

There is no need to pursue the comparison further, for I do not wish to disparage Drink-water's poem, of which I thought highly when I was young. But enough has been said, I hope, to indicate, even to those unconverted to Eliot, what such a conversion involves and why, once the mind and method behind " The Hollow Men " is appreciated, it is impossible to return to the nebulous versifying of our latter-day romantics.

The division of literary works into " classic " and " romantic " has been deplored. Admittedly it is an over-simplification, corresponding to the political division of Conservative and Liberal, which contains many easily-detected anomalies. The right-wing Liberal, for instance —the Whig—is much more " conservative " than the Tory-Democrat, and is actually closer to his Die-Hard antagonists than to the Radicals of his own party. So in recent English poetry, the last great romantic, Elroy Flecker, by his enthusiasm for the Parnassians, betrayed definite classical leanings, while the first great classicist,

T. S. Eliot, by his attachment to the Symbolists,
is not altogether free from romanticism. Such
considerations certainly suggest a case for the
abolition of labels. It is a worthy argument,
except that it can end only in the admission of
the simple fact that every poet has individual
idiosyncrasies. The broad division remains
necessary, after all.

" Romantic " and " classical " are, indeed,
so valuable because they are indicative of the
main tendencies in every personal experience.
In ourselves we feel both the duty of obedience
to tradition and the urge for individual assertion ; the spirit which affirms and the spirit
which denies ; the simultaneous need for con-
formity and nonconformity. And each one will
give his final allegiance to whichever cause he
feels to be the more important. But he must
choose. He cannot escape the label. The
romantic is in general the rebel, the individualist,
the liberal, the protestant. The classicist is the
authoritarian, the traditionalist, the conservative,
the catholic. The division enters every depart-

ment of life. So Æschylus is classical and
Euripides romantic ; Julius Cæsar romantic and
Marcus Brutus classical ; St. Bernard of Clair-
vaux classical and Peter Abélard romantic ;
Michael Angelo romantic and Leonardo da
Vinci classical ; Ignatius Loyola classical and
Martin Luther romantic ; Shakespeare romantic
and Dante classical ; Wellington classical and
Nelson romantic ; Disraeli romantic and Glad-
stone classical ; Cézanne classical and Van
Gogh romantic ; D. H. Lawrence romantic
and James Joyce classical.

To these dangerous generalisations I will add
one more.   The *great* romantic is usually superior
in achievement and influence to the great classicist ; he has the superabundant vitality which
can both create and rebel and he has the more
profound vision.   But minor classicists, even at
their worst, are saved by that very Form which
the individualist overthrows from the pointless
inanity into which minor romantics degenerate.

It is this degeneration which has made the
return to classicism inevitable.   Subjectivity has

resulted in anarchy. It is quite true that a romantic like Wordsworth made the expression of his individual belief, as in the " Ode on the Intimations of Immortality," fulfil the function of great poetry far more truly than the uninspired formalism of the classicists of his day, however objectively they might endeavour to " justify the ways of God to man." It is true that Byron could interest a continent in his own tempestuous character or Swinburne startle a nation by his vision of vice. They could be personal because they possessed personality. But by the petty preoccupations of the " Georgians " we are not amused. We must have some standard other than their private eccentricities, some philosophy other than their limited apprehensions, some method of communication other than their worn-out words.

This was realised, of course, by some members of the school themselves. Elroy Flecker, in his defence of the Parnassians, wrote : " To be didactic like Wordsworth, to write dull poems of unwieldy length, to bury like Tennyson or

Browning poetry of exquisite beauty in monstrous realms of vulgar, feeble or obscure versifying, to overlay fine work with gross and irrelevant egoism like Victor Hugo, would be abhorrent, and rightly so, to members of this school. . . . Read the works of Hérédia, if you would understand how conscious and perfect artistry, far from stifling inspiration, fashions it into shapes of unimaginable beauty. . . . At the present moment there can be no doubt that English poetry stands in need of some such saving doctrine to redeem it from the formlessness and the didactic tendencies which are now in fashion.''

This passage is valuable because it shows so clearly the reason both for Flecker's success as a minor poet and for his failure to become a major one. He is conscious of the need for objectivity, but he confines it to a creation of a limited '' poetic '' beauty. He will create a world independent of '' gross and irrelevant egoisms,'' but that world still has little connection with the real world in which he lived. He

was essentially an " escapist." The opening
lines of his " Prayer " :

> " Let me not know how sins and sorrows glide
> Along the sombre city of our rage,
> Or why the sons of men are heavy-eyed,"

at once reveal and condemn ; so that although,
with one hand, by his careful craftsmanship and
his insistence on form, he gave a new life to
romantic poetry, with the other, by his narrow
definition of " beauty " and limitation of the
scope of subjects it might illumine, he made the
gift of little effect.

Second only to Flecker in popular esteem was
Rupert Brooke. Brooke's approach was the
exact opposite to Flecker's. He wished to en-
large the scope of subjects with which poetry
might deal, while at the same time jealously
retaining a personal approach. He admitted
that he was unrepentant for introducing " un-
pleasant " themes into his verse, and in his
effort to do so, he brought " prosaic " words
into poetry, much to poetry's enrichment.

Flecker could write with a perfection of simplicity :

" It was so old a ship—who knows, who knows ?
    —And yet so beautiful, I watched in vain
    To see the mast burst open with a rose
    And the whole deck put on its leaves again,"

and Brooke, with enthusiastic sincerity :

" The damned ship lurched and slithered. Quiet
        and quick
    My cold gorge rose ; the long sea rolled ;
    I knew
    I must think hard of something, or be sick ;
    And could think hard of only one thing—*you!*"

The difference here between the " I " of Flecker and the " I " of Brooke sufficiently indicates the objective and subjective approaches, whereas a comparison of the words shows the extent to which the younger poet had brought a breath of life into the heavy atmosphere of " escapist " verse. And although to-day we may consider a sonnet on sea-sickness to be just rather a pity, at the time the theme was undoubtedly a portent.

Yet neither Flecker nor Brooke could give

poetry the lead it awaited. For that there was
needed a combination of their talents. To say
that their younger contemporary, T. S. Eliot,
was to offer this, was to fuse Brooke's realism
with Flecker's formalism, is to give far too
superficial an impression of Eliot's achievement.
He did so much more than that. The observation, however, is worth making, because it
helps to establish some connection between the
old school and the new. Eliot cannot be
approached *merely* by way of the Georgians ; he
has been too susceptible to French and American
influences, to Laforgue and Gautier and Ezra
Pound ; but, for the Plain Reader, the English
approach is not altogether barred.

It is worth noting, too, that two of Eliot's
enthusiasms—Webster and the late Elizabethan
dramatists ; Donne and the Metaphysical poets
—had also been " rediscovered " by Rupert
Brooke. The very fact that they needed " re-
discovering " was, of course, an indication of
the barrenness of the Romantic tradition, which,
had it remembered Webster, would have avoided

its thinness of word-texture and, had it remembered Donne, would not have excluded from
its content thought and wit. Yet Brooke failed
to use what he had found. He knew, for
instance, that Webster perpetually plagiarised—
that, to take one example, a famous passage in
" The Duchess of Malfi " is composed entirely
of extracts from Sidney's " Arcadia "—but he
saw this phenomenon only as an interesting
fact for criticism. Being a romantic, he was
too concerned with his individual perceptions
to regard such wholesale plagiarism as anything
more than a somewhat ungentlemanly form of
cribbing in exams. Eliot, on the other hand,
saw in it one of the means by which his poetry
could be made to approximate to " a living
whole of all the poetry that has ever been
written."

Even what little Brooke did borrow, he spoilt
in the borrowing. He could understand the
necessity for introducing " prosaic " words into
verse ; he could not understand the use of
words which, while vaguely " poetic," were

yet indicative of thought and evocative of concrete images. Thus he took an epithet from
Donne's :

" For, nor in nothing, nor in things
    Extreme, and scatt'ring bright, can love inhere ; "

and transplanted it in :

" When Beauty and Beauty meet
    All naked, fair to fair,
    The earth is crying-sweet
    And scattering-bright the air."

The contrast is the measure of his failure.

Not only Brooke, but nearly every " Georgian " suffers from a plethora of adjectives.
When words become worn out, this is inevitable. Adjectival emphasis, the prerogative of
the adolescent and the uneducated, is also a
mark of senility and the failure of inspiration.
Ivy is useful for concealing bad workmanship
and may impart to undistinguished architecture
a spurious romantic " beauty " ; but ivy would
intolerably mar a building of classical perfection. When the imagery of a poem is no
longer clear, the decoration of it merely assists

c

its haziness. The addition of words decreases
its meaning.

Again, it may be useful to take an example—
two translations of the same chorus from the
" Bacchæ " of Euripides. The first by Professor Gilbert Murray, the second by " H. D." :

" Will they ever come to me, ever again,
        The long long dances,
    On through the dark till the dim stars wane ?
    Shall I feel the dew on my throat, and the stream
    Of wind in my hair ? Shall our white feet gleam
        In the dim expanses ?
    Oh, feet of a fawn to the greenwood fled,
        Alone in the grass and the loveliness ;
    Leap of the hunted, no more in dread,
        Beyond the snares and the deadly press :
    Yet a voice still in the distance sounds,
    A voice and a fear and a haste of hounds ;
    O wildly labouring, fiercely fleet,
        Onward yet by river and glen . . .
    Is it joy or terror, ye storm-swift feet ? . . .
        To the dear lone lands untroubled of men,
    Where no voice sounds, and amid the shadowy
        green
    The little things of the woodland live unseen.

    What else is Wisdom ? What of man's endeavour
        Or God's high grace, so lovely and so great ?

To stand from fear set free, to breathe and wait ;
To hold a hand uplifted over Hate ;
And shall not Loveliness be loved for ever ? ''

and

" Again,
    again in the night,
    shall I beat white feet in delight
    of the dance
    to Dionysos ?
    shall I bear my throat to the night
    air
    and the dew in the night ?
    again shall my pulses beat
    like the deer
    escaped from the net,
    from the knots
    and the huntsman's shouts,
    from the hounds
    and the hunting riot ?
    shall I lie in the meadows sweet,
    escaped,
    escaped from the lot
    of men,
    like a faun in the desert,
    like a wind
    by the river bank ?
    again,
    again
    shall I rest

ecstatic in loneliness,
apart in the haunted forest,
hidden by leaf
and leaf-branch?
O which of the gifts of the gods
is the best gift?
this,
this,
this,
this ;
escape
from the power of the hunting pack,
and to know that wisdom is best
and beauty
sheer holiness."

There is no question which is nearer to the Greek, or which the stronger and cleaner. Professor Murray, faced with the problem of introducing the classics to a romantic age, had to evolve a fashionable paraphrase. " H. D.," an Imagist, restores something of the Classic simplicity without loss of understanding.

Thus the Imagists, by another path, had made an effort to escape from the Romantic doom. They insisted on the clarity which comes from the use of definite images, and on a measure of

objectivity. They had much in common with
Flecker, but went further in their careful choice
of the exact word, while on the other hand they
allowed more latitude in stanza-form and rhythm.
But they made his mistake of excluding from
their verse whole tracts of contemporary life
and problems. They, too, were " escapists."

There is one more manifestation to be noticed
—those experimenters with free verse who followed subjectivity to its logical conclusion of
anarchy and brought to poetry not only the
language of prose, but also its formlessness.
With them the disintegration of romanticism
was complete.

The reason for the failure of these efforts was
that each devoted itself to one part of the
problem without considering the whole. What
was needed was a return to tradition as well as
an enlargement of the scope of subject matter ;
a greater economy of word as well as a greater
flexibility of rhythm ; a depersonalisation of
outlook as well as minute observation. These
things T. S. Eliot was to give to English poetry,

with the result that, in the words of Mr. F. R. Leavis, "in his work by 1920 English poetry had made a new start."

To sum the matter up, if we accept the well-known definition of poetry as "the concrete and artistic expression of the human mind in emotional and rhythmical language," we may say that, with our latter-day romantics, it had lost its concreteness, the meaning of "artistic" had been limited, a personal and partial perception had been substituted for "the human mind," its emotional currency had been so debased that it was almost valueless and its rhythm had been either stereotyped or surrendered.

Adequately to sustain this thesis would need a lengthy series of individual critical examinations which would be out of place here. I have given no more than the barest hints, which the reader may test for himself by referring to almost any anthology of Georgian verse. My concern with these things is only in their bearing on T. S. Eliot's practice and theory of poetry.

IV

T. S. Eliot's Theory of Poetry

"POETRY is not a turning loose of emotion, but an escape from emotion ; it is not the expression of personality, but an escape from personality." Thus Eliot, challengingly, in his essay on "Tradition and the Individual Talent," in which he outlines his "programme for the *métier* of poetry,". an essay which forms, necessarily, the basis of this chapter.

The first requisite of the poet is the historical sense, involving a realisation of the meaning of tradition. It is this sense which "compels a man to write not merely with his own generation in his bones, but with a feeling that the whole of the literature of Europe from Homer and within it the whole of the literature of his own country has a simultaneous existence and composes a simultaneous order." This is neither

so difficult nor so revolutionary as it sounds.
On a lower plane it is partially achieved by most
of us. We may consider that Shakespeare was
an Elizabethan dramatist now dead, and announce
that we have " no use " for him, but that will
not prevent us quoting jocularly " To be or
not to be," or to feel insulted if we are referred
to as " Shylock." We may have never read
Homer, and yet have very decided opinions
about Helen of Troy. We may be exceedingly
hazy about the century in which Dante lived,
and yet describe a battlefield as an " inferno."
We may never have even heard the name of
Cervantes, and yet recognise a quixotic action.
In this very superficial way, Homer and Shakespeare and Dante and Cervantes enjoy a " simultaneous existence " even to the " man-in-the-
street," who is certainly not interested in them
and would never dream of reading anything
they wrote.

The intelligent reader of poetry will go one
step farther. Besides being familiar with the
general outlines of the great works of the past,

he will appreciate more allusions. When Mr.
Galsworthy begins a poem :

> " Come, let us lay a crazy lance at rest
>   And tilt at windmills under a wild sky,"

he will not immediately deplore the amount of
erudition necessary to recognise the reference to
" Don Quixote," just as when Keats introduces
in his " Ode to a Nightingale " :

> " the sad heart of Ruth, when sick for home
> She stood in tears amid the alien corn,"

we do not accuse him of pedantry because he
assumes our acquaintance with an irrelevant
Hebrew legend. Yet many accuse Eliot of it
when, in the " nightingale passage " of " The
Waste Land," he assumes a similar knowledge
of a relevant Greek myth. And if we do not
immediately recognise the entrance of the Inferno
in the lines :

> " Those who have crossed
> With direct eyes, to death's other Kingdom
> Remember us—if at all—not as lost
> Violent souls, but only
> As the hollow men
> The stuffed men,"

we are apt to disparage Eliot's knowledge, instead of our own lack of it. There is, obviously, no reason for this. It is due to a limitation of our personal reading, an admission that we know the "Book of Ruth" better than Ovid's "Metamorphoses," and "Don Quixote" better than the "Divine Comedy."

Yet we have no right (nor, if we pause a moment for thought, shall we claim it) to impose our limitations on the poet, the "maker." For the poet is at the third stage, as far above the critic as the critic is above the "man-in-the-street." And he, as Eliot insists, must be acquainted with the whole of living literature, because it is a necessary part of his contemporary experience.

The *whole* of living literature ? That must be qualified by an admission of human limitations. The whole of *living* literature ? That involves a critical elimination, about which one could wrangle till doomsday. But to argue what is or what is not "living" would be profitless here. I shall give (without necessarily endorsing) the list which Ezra Pound offers as

" the result of twenty-seven years' thought on the subject." His choice is the more useful because it seems to correspond roughly with Eliot's own reading, a fact not altogether surprising when we remember the friendship between the two poets ("The Waste Land" is "For Ezra Pound, *il miglior fabbro*," and Eliot sponsored Pound's poems in England).

Pound's "minimum basis for a sound and liberal education in letters" is Confucius ; Homer ; Ovid, Catullus and Propertius ; the Troubadours and Minnesingers ; Dante and his circle ; Villon ; Voltaire's critical writings ; Stendhal ; Flaubert ; Gautier, Corbière and Rimbaud. These are works of the first intensity, of the "masters" who "either start with a core of their own and accumulate adjuncts, or digest a vast mass of subject-matter, apply a number of known modes of expression, and succeed in pervading the whole with some special quality or some special character of their own, and bring the whole to a state of homogeneous fulness." This minimum will, of course, be

increased by the addition of many great writers
of lesser intensity, who are certainly " living,"
though perhaps less " alive." Englishmen, too,
must be presumed to know their own literature.

Now this body of work, according to Eliot,
will, for the poet (and therefore, to a lesser
extent, for the reader of poetry), " compose a
simultaneous order." Consequently, whenever
a new work of art arrives, " the *whole* existing
order must be, if ever so slightly, altered ; and
so the relations, proportions, values of each
work of art toward the whole are readjusted."

This process is easily illustrated by reference
to Pound's list. Each of the writers he mentions brought into existence something which
was not in the world before. The civilisation
which knew only Homer lacked a vision and a
sensibility which the civilisation which knew
both Homer and Dante possessed. But the
work of Dante in no way invalidated the work
of Homer ; it only altered its significance,
modified it by relating it to the new thing.
What is true of a civilisation is true of the

individual, and a similar modification works on
a smaller scale.   Thus the poetry of Eliot himself has altered the order of English poetry for
the reader.   For instance, in 1932 the relative
values of (say) Milton and Dryden or of Tennyson and Thomas Hardy are quite different from
those accepted in 1902.   And this readjustment
is not due to the passing of time : it is due to
the creation of new art.

Once this view of tradition is understood, the
relation of the individual poet to it becomes
clear.   On the one hand, he cannot simply re-
state it (which is what the majority of verse
writers do), for then his work " would not be
new, and would therefore not be a work of
art."   On the other, he obviously cannot ignore
it, cannot " innovate illogically," with no reference to it.   " True originality is merely development ; and if it is right development it
may appear in the end so *inevitable* that we
almost come to the point of view of denying
all ' original ' virtue to the poet."

This, the first step in Eliot's theory, will not,

I imagine, be seriously disputed. It is what this theory involves when applied to the practice of poetry that has aroused such furious opposition. For it means that the poet, because throughout his career he is developing the consciousness of the living past, must therefore surrender " himself as he is at the moment to something which is more valuable." So " the progress of an artist is a continual self-sacrifice, a continual extinction of personality."

This *extinction of personality* is a cardinal heresy to the great majority of people who imagine that a poet's first duty is to " look into his heart and write." A heresy, too, even if they accept Eliot's retort that " that is not looking deep enough. . . . One must look into the cerebral cortex, the nervous system, and the digestive tracts." They will grant that literature is as much a part of experience as the incidental happenings of daily life ; they will even admit that the customary distinction between " life " and " literature " may have to be revised, so that the fact that a man stumps his toe on getting out of his morning bath shall not be considered more relevant or " real " than the fact that, while in it, he was declaiming extracts from " Hamlet." Yet they will resolutely refuse to allow that the first duty of a poet is to become depersonalised.

To explain this depersonalisation more fully, Eliot uses the scientific analogy of a catalyst. But before examining that, it may be useful to inquire a little further into the reason of the romantic preoccupation with " personality." For just as we have seen that the objection to erudition is not at all an objection to learning as such, but only an illogical annoyance that the poet's scholarship is greater than ours, so we may find that our dislike of depersonalisation has equally flimsy foundations. It is surely a fallacy to suppose that, because an emotion is strongly felt, *therefore* it is bound to be communicated strongly ; that the genuineness of an experience is some sort of guarantee of genuine art in its expression. As much emotion lies behind the poor jingle of an amateur rhymester as behind the most sublime masterpiece, and the beginner's failure to communicate that emotion to the reader is due not in the least to the poverty of his feelings or his lack of " personality," but to the insufficiency of his art. The great actor who moves vast audiences to pity or to terror is not himself moved. Indeed, it is, in the main, true to say that the extent to which he can move his audience depends on the extent to which he can remain unmoved and therefore free to concentrate his attention on his technical means of communication. This may be lamentable to the romantically-minded who are partial to " Pagliacci," but it is surely logical enough.

For the poet, as for the actor, " emotions which he has never experienced will serve his turn as well as those familiar to him." " The business of the poet is not to find new emotions, but to use the ordinary ones and, in working them up into poetry, to express feelings which are not in actual emotions at all." Also " it is not in his personal emotions, the emotions provoked by particular events in his life, that the poet is in any way remarkable or interesting."

How, then, is emotion to be communicated in poetry ? Eliot has answered that question quite simply : "The only way of expressing emotion in the form of art is by finding an 'objective correlative' ; in other words, a set of objects, a situation, a chain of events which shall be the formula of that *particular* emotion ; such that when the external facts, which must terminate in sensory experience, are given, the emotion is immediately evoked." As the whole of his work offers an example of this mode of expression, it is hardly necessary to single out any particular passage. But one may ask, in passing, whether the ennui, the aimlessness, the futility of an existence devoted to the fulfilment of social obligations, a career of calls and parties and small talk, have ever been better communicated than in that most famous of Eliot's single lines :

" I have measured out my life with coffee spoons " ?

There, surely, the perfect "objective correlative" is found.

D

If these conclusions be accepted—and, frankly, I do not see how they can be avoided—they strike a death-blow at subjective romanticism. It means that a " Sonnet on Reflections inspired by the Body of a Dead Frog found by me during a Walking Tour " (which might conveniently epitomise the " Georgian " verse of the " Squirearchy ") need no longer be seriously considered as a contribution to poetry, whatever its value to psychology. It means that we must revise our definition of a poet. So we return to the catalyst.

" When a bit of finely filiated platinum is introduced into a chamber containing oxygen and sulphur dioxide . . . the two gases . . . form sulphurous acid. This combination takes place only if the platinum is present ; nevertheless the newly formed acid contains no trace of platinum, and the platinum itself is apparently unaffected ; has remained inert, neutral, unchanged. The mind of the poet is the shred of platinum." Or again, " The poet's mind is, in fact, a receptacle for seizing and storing up numberless feelings, phrases, images, which remain there until all the particles which can unite to form a new compound are present together." These "feelings, phrases, images" are drawn partly from the works of poets of the past—that is, traditional experience—and partly from the individual experience of the writer. For, of course, depersonalisation does not deny individual experience—it merely insists that " the more perfect the artist, the more completely separate in him will be the man who suffers and the mind which creates."

To put it another way : " The mind of the mature poet differs from that of the immature one not precisely in any valuation of ' personality,' not being necessarily more interesting or having ' more to say,' but rather by being a more finely perfected medium in which special or very varied feelings are at liberty to enter into new combinations."

The more " finely perfected " the mind, the more subtle—in a good sense—will be the poetry. That is inevitable, for it is the hardest thing in the world to communicate with any

exactitude even a simple emotion. The refusal
to recognise this elementary fact is the fallacy
at the root of a third objection to Eliot's poetry
—objection to its " difficulty." It is popularly
assumed that great art is always " simple "—
that is to say, immediately intelligible to every-
body. (So Democracy flatters itself. The truth
is rather in Stendhal's remark that it takes
eighty years for anything to reach the general
public.) But art is never simple in that sense,
and the belief that it is is based on the curious
dogma of the infallibility of language. Just as
no one—to quote Mr. Chesterton—" believes
that an ordinary civilised stockbroker can really
produce out of his own inside noises which denote
all the mysteries of memory and all the agonies
of desire," so no one acquainted, even superficially, with poetry would really wish to sustain
the thesis that " difficulty " denotes inferiority.

It is quite true certainly that Homer is much
less complex than Shakespeare, but that is
because the civilisation for which he wrote, the
range of its knowledge and its interests, were

smaller. And the difference between the age of Shakespeare and the age of Homer is not greater than that between ourselves and the Elizabethans. "It appears likely," says Eliot, "that poets in our civilisation, as it exists at present, must be *difficult*. Our civilisation comprehends great variety and complexity, and this variety and complexity, playing upon a refined sensibility, must produce various and complex results. The poet must become more and more comprehensive, more allusive, more indirect, in order to force, to dislocate if necessary, language into his meaning."

There are many ways in which this forcing, this dislocation can be effected. One is by the use of "the element of *surprise* so essential to poetry." This early critical dictum of Eliot's might be taken as affording one line of approach to his own work. One might even say that his technique is based on a series of surprises of a certain and specialised sort. In the first lines of his first volume we get it :

" Let us go then, you and I,
    When the evening is spread out against the sky. . ."

Here is a lyrical, " romantic " opening, crying for the colours of the sunset in its third line. The third line is :

" Like a patient etherised upon a table."

The very shock of it, by arresting the reader, makes communication possible. Had the line contained a conventional image, it would have passed unnoticed ; we should have vaguely ascribed to the sunset our own familiar and half-conscious sentimentalisings, without troubling about the poet's meaning. But the etherised patient gives at once the sense of doom, the troubled excitement and the nameless fear of the hour when the sun goes out. The sun will rise again to-morrow : the patient is only etherised, not dead. Or again, the anæsthetic simile, with its reminiscence of the gradual loss of consciousness, suggests the slow, imperceptible conquest of the dark. And the anæsthetic is followed by the operation. We see the gaping wound, the streams of red blood making crazy, inconsequent patterns on the inert body as the red light flows across the immovable sky. Both the atmosphere and the visual image of sunset are thus suggested by the figure. But there is even more in it. The comparison could not have been made a hundred years ago ; by focussing the contemporary consciousness, it stimulates whole series of reactions which are generally thought to be " unpoetic." (" Poetry," as Pound says, " is still considered by a great number of drivelling imbeciles synonymous with ' lofty and flowery language.' ")

Here, then, is a very simple illustration in practice of the theory quoted at the beginning of the chapter : " Poetry is not a turning loose of emotion, but an escape from emotion ; it is not the expression of personality, but an escape from personality." Eliot is not emotionally concerned about the fate of the patient, nor does he betray a personality morbidly interested in operations. Escaping from both emotion and personality, he has succeeded in communicating to the reader a very complex emotion in a line stamped with the personality of his age.

The introduction of the " contemporary consciousness " raises the problem of what is meant
by modernity. " It is almost too platitudinous
to say," writes Eliot, " that one is not modern
by writing about chimney-pots, or archaic by
writing about oriflammes." Unfortunately it
is exactly that platitude which is usually forgotten. Most " modern " novels, for example,
do not express anything peculiarly modern ;
they deal with aspects of life which are common to every age, but which our predecessors
had the taste to take for granted. That sort of
modernity is the reverse of " modern." The
genuine " modern " will be extraordinarily conscious of those particular moments in the living
past which correspond most nearly to the situation in the living present. He will then ensure
that his work modifies the traditional order by
shifting the emphasis on to those moments.
Eliot's " surprise " technique, for instance, is
not something which he invented out of his
own head, but something which he found in
the work of the Metaphysical poets. So, by

the simple process of reading Eliot's poems, we
become aware that Donne is more " modern "
than Tennyson ; that the " Hymne to God my
God, in my Sicknesse," expresses more accurately
than " Crossing the Bar " the temper of our
epoch.

Of course, in order to get certain traditional
effects as well as to evoke certain unique features
of the time, it is necessary to have recourse to
contemporary idiom—as in the anæsthetic simile.
But it is not simply the use of the idiom that
makes modernity, and it is surprising how com-
paratively rare such images are in Eliot's work.
In his 1930 volume, " Ash Wednesday," there
are none at all. And " Ash Wednesday " is
quite as " modern " as anything he has written.
The Machine Age need not be expressed only
by machine images (though Eliot has given us
at least one memorable one—the few moments
before the end of the clerk's working-day

" when the human engine waits
Like a taxi throbbing waiting.")

The truth is rather that it will be expressed by

new *rhythms*—a train of thought to which Eliot has supplied the clue in the sentence : " Perhaps the conditions of modern life (think how large a part is now played in our sensory life by the internal combustion engine !) have altered our perception of rhythms," and which need not be examined in detail. But it may be worth suggesting this : any man who, in a railway carriage, sits in a half-doze listening to the wheels go round, noting both the regularity of the beat and the perpetual modifications of the regularity, the quickening and the slackening, or who looks out of the window to see the strange rising and falling of the telegraph wires as the poles fly past, will have more essential knowledge of rhythm and will be able better to appreciate it in modern poetry than the student who has pored over every book on metre which has ever been written.

Thus it is in the rhythms and in the complex emotions, expressed partly by new idioms but mainly by a readjustment of tradition, that we shall find evidence of Eliot's modernity—some-

thing very different from an attempt to be
" modern " by writing sonnets about sewing-
machines.

Take, for example, that symptom of our
times, the evening newspaper, with its timid
appeal to the common measure of democratic
intelligence, and the consequent nostalgia for
the past it excites in men of sensibility—for the
time when those who could read could also feel
and understand things worthy to be written.
This, and much more, is compressed in four
lines of an early poem :

> " I mount the steps and ring the bell, turning
>   Wearily, as one would turn to nod good-bye to
>   Rochefoucauld,
>   If the street were time and he at the end of the
>   street,
>   And I say, ' Cousin Harriet, here is the *Boston
>   Evening Transcript.*' "

It might be objected that the " I " here is
purely personal, and that Eliot is merely expressing his individual reaction which *happens* to
coincide with the reaction of those of a similar
temperament—in other words, that he has fallen

into the subjectivity which he deplores. But
surely the introduction of Rochefoucauld is
sufficient answer. By recalling the French wit
and his civilisation, he has created a situation
independent of his personal attitude and made
the " I " a general term indicative of the tens
of millions of wage-earners in every country
who come home at eventide and present a copy
of the evening paper to their waiting relatives.

It will be noticed how the emotion consequent
on the thought is reinforced by a change of
rhythm. As Eliot's mastery of his medium increases, he secures, by his brilliant contrasts, his
suggestive transitions, and his subtle rhythms,
even more complex effects with even greater
economy. Yet, however complicated his poems
may seem at first reading, they rest on the funda-
mentals of the theory we have examined. They
express contemporary consciousness in a depersonalised manner by a reference to tradition.
They communicate their emotion by presenting
an " objective correlative " based on both past
literature and present experience.

V

The Early Poems (1917 and 1920)

§ 1. " *Prufrock and other Observations* "

" TO read ' The Love Song of J. Alfred
Prufrock ' or ' Portrait of a Lady ' is
pure delight, surpassing the combined pleasures—
if they could be combined—of Henry James's
subtle analysis and George Meredith's ironical
humour." That is not the challenging opinion
of a young admirer, but the considered judgment
of so conservative a critic as Sir Henry Newbolt.

When Eliot wrote " Portrait of a Lady " he
was twenty-one ; " Prufrock " followed a year
later; and in 1912 came " La Figlia che Piange."
These, with " Conversation Galante," the
earliest poem which he has allowed to be
printed, form the love-verses of the young poet.
The description may sound fantastic, but I have
used it deliberately to emphasise again the shock

caused by the impact of Eliot on the world of romantic poetry.

Rupert Brooke at twenty-three sobbed :

" I said I splendidly loved you ; it's not true.
　　Such long swift tides stir not a land-locked sea.
　　On gods and fools the high risk falls—on you—
　　　The clean clear bitter-sweet that's not for me,"

but T. S. Eliot at nineteen had given us :

" And I then : ' Someone frames upon the keys
　　That exquisite nocturne, with which we explain
　　The night and moonshine ; music which we
　　　seize
　　To body forth our vacuity.'
　　　She then : ' Does this refer to me ? '
　　' Oh no, it is I who am inane.' "

Brooke, obviously, was understandable : *that* kind of love-lament, at his age, very right and proper ; but Eliot, surely, was—to say the least —precocious !

To-day, with some knowledge of Eliot's theory of poetry, the reader will find the volume " Prufrock and Other Observations " less surprising, though even in 1917, when it was published, the title " Observations " should have allayed false hopes. It was the poet's observation, in part directed with uncanny detachment on his own youthful emotions, which enabled him at twenty-two to give us the picture of a middle-aged man, hesitating on the brink of a love-affair and finally refusing to surrender himself for fear of appearing ridiculous.

> " And indeed there will be time
> To wonder ' Do I dare ? ' and, ' Do I dare ? '
> Time to turn back and descend the stair,
> With a bald spot in the middle of my hair—
> (They will say : ' How his hair is growing thin ! ')
> My morning coat, my collar mounting firmly to
>   the chin,
> My necktie rich and modest, but asserted by a
>   simple pin—
> (They will say : ' But how his arms and legs are
>   thin ! ')
> Do I dare
> Disturb the universe ? "

Something more than the fear of the ridiculous deters Alfred J. Prufrock, however. Past experience has brought both disillusion and wisdom. For wisdom consists in recognising the things in life which are impossible :

" No ! I am not Prince Hamlet, nor was meant to
    be ;
  Am an attendant lord, one that will do
  To swell a progress, start a scene or two . . ."

And disillusion only means realising that the
individual's road to happiness may not in the
least coincide with the course recommended by
general opinion. Already, in " Portrait of a
Lady," he expressed this with clear brevity :

  " the smell of hyacinths across the garden
    Recalling things that other people have desired,"

and in " Prufrock " the reiterated :

  " And would it have been worth it, after all,
    Would it have been worth while ? "

demands an inevitable negative.

  " Portrait of a Lady " reverses the situation
of " Prufrock." Here it is the woman who is
middle-aged, endeavouring to attract a man
younger than herself—an unforgettable portrait,
which, in spite of its cruelty, never degenerates
into caricature. The conversation of the lady,
at once so natural that it might be dialogue
in a good play and so revealing that it might

grace some psychological novel, at the same time
remains fine poetry. Eliot's gift for the vivid
and exact phrase is already apparent—the room
with its "atmosphere of Juliet's tomb";
the foreign pianist who can "transmit the
Preludes, through his hair and finger-tips";
the lady herself "slowly twisting the lilac
stalks," her voice

> "like the insistent out-of-tune
> Of a broken violin on an August afternoon,"

and the man's failure to cope with the situation :

> "My self-possession gutters; we are really in the
> dark,"

while the technical device of revealing two
characters by the conversation of the one and the
answering, but unspoken, comment of the other
is hardly less successful here than in the later
and more famous example of it in "The Waste
Land."

These love-poems, too, deal with exactly the
same feelings as do their romantic counterparts.
"The pangs of despised love," much the same
at any age, are usually expressed by the young

E

in directly personal verse, whereas Eliot, in allowing the creating mind to examine the sufferings of the man, has merely transferred them to the rejected heroine of the " Portrait." He has found there his " objective correlative." In the same way, the timidity and gaucherie inseparable from first love are utilised for the diffident Prufrock. Eliot, in short, is writing lyric poems ; but he is using his material for them in the manner of a dramatist.

From the personal relationship of man and woman, Eliot turned to examine the world in general, and in " Preludes," " Rhapsody on a Windy Night " and " Morning at the Window " we are given the reactions of a sensitive man seeking beauty and finding ugliness, seeking order and finding chaos. Revolted by his discovery of disorganised drabness on every side, he insists relentlessly that his readers see it also. He makes it quite clear that if the individual can gain no lasting satisfaction from love, the citizen can gain less from society. Civilisation is :

" A broken spring in a factory yard,
    Rust that clings to the form that the strength has
      left
    Hard and curled and ready to snap."

Then, for two years, it seems, Eliot was silent. At any rate, the last section of the first volume, containing the short acid comments on Boston society (a society " refined beyond the point of civilisation "), belong to the year 1915. These poems, " The Boston Evening Transcript," " Aunt Helen," " Cousin Nancy " and " Mr. Apollinax," are on the borderland of the sneer. They are saved from this reproach only by the detachment given them by their allusive background, for in them Eliot first definitely develops the technique of the contrasted past and present. Actually, when read in the light of later poems, they represent rather an unsuccessful effort to be unconcerned, the short lull between the pained disillusion of the early period and the savage anger which was to follow.

Before considering the 1920 volume, however, it may be well to mention the masters on whom the young poet was modelling himself. There is

no secrecy about it. He has told us frankly
that the form in which he began to write was
directly drawn from the study of Laforgue
together with the later Elizabethan drama. It
is *vers libre*, but hardly free verse, as we have
come to understand the term. "The *vers libre*
of Jules Laforgue," says Eliot, " is free verse
in much the way that the later verse of Shakespeare, Webster and Tourneur, is free verse :
that is to say, it stretches, contracts and distorts
the traditional French measure as later Elizabethan
and Jacobean poetry stretches, contracts and distorts the blank verse measure."

Laforgue and Webster influenced more than
the form of the poems. Laforgue determined
many of the images and the general manner of
treatment, while the Elizabethans enriched the
word texture. Though parallels between Laforgue and Eliot are numerous, they are not,
except for the academic mind, particularly
interesting, nor is there any merit in the discovery of them. Those who wish to pursue the
subject will find guidance in M. René Taupin's

"Influence du Symbolisme Français sur la Poësie Americaine de 1910 à 1920." Here it is sufficient to suggest a comparison between "La Figlia che Piange" and "Sur une Défunte," between the ending of "Prufrock" and the ending of "Légende," between "Conversation Galante" and "Autre Complainte de Lord Pierrot" and other poems ; to notice the similarity of mannerisms—"the repetitions of words pedantically long," as Laforgue's

> "Et que jamais soit tout, bien intrinsèquement,
>   Très hermétiquement, primordialement"

and Eliot's

> "And all its relations
>   Its divisions and precisions"—

and to remind the reader that certain lines of Laforgue are translated or adapted by Eliot, such as "simple et sans foi comme un bonjour" becoming "simple and faithless as a smile and shake of the hand," or

> "Là, voyons, Mam'zelle la Lune
>   Ne gardons pas ainsi rancune"

becoming

> " Regard the moon,
>   La lune ne garde aucune rancune."

The important resemblance is not so much in details as in atmosphere and approach. To quote M. Taupin, "for Eliot, as for Laforgue, the problem was to be able to cover with cultivated modernity the chronicle or the diary of a man of his time with the proper décor of the time."

Laforgue, of course, does not stand alone. There is also Corbière, whose influence, though less, is not lacking. There are Baudelaire and Verlaine and Mallarmé. And in the next volume, the 1920 poems, there is very much Gautier. The relevance of Corbière perhaps is as a link, standing as he does, historically, between Gautier and Laforgue. What the latter is to Eliot's work between 1911 and 1915, the former is to the period 1917 to 1920. Between the first and the second volume there is a definite break in technique as well as in temper. The new temper is Eliot's own ; but the technique deriving from Gautier is in great measure due to Ezra Pound.

§ 2. *"Poems, 1920."*

The association with Pound, which was to influence all Eliot's later work, began at this point. Together the two poets read and studied the same sources, interchanged ideas, and made similar experiments in versification. But each retained his individuality. In Pound's case the result was "Mauberley"; in Eliot's the satirical Sweeney poems. Their combined authority checked the movement towards verse which was becoming anarchic rather than free, and they revived the strict quatrain of Gautier, while making, within the limits of it, continual modification of rhythm. Thus Eliot :

> " The lengthened shadow of a man
>   Is history, said Emerson,
> Who had not seen the silhouette
>   Of Sweeney straddled in the sun."

and Pound :

> " All things are a flowing,
>   Sage Heracleitus says ;
> But a tawdry cheapness
>   Shall outlast our days."

There was, however, one important difference between them. Eliot was all the time concerned chiefly with what he said, whereas Pound was more interested in how he said it. It is this, finally, which establishes Eliot's superiority. No one has given to Pound more enthusiastic and generous praise than has Eliot, and of " Mauberley " itself he asserts that " this book would be, were it nothing else, a text-book of modern versification." The unfortunate thing is that to many of us it seems exactly that and very little more. Eliot may acknowledge Pound as his master, but we cannot, though we must certainly admit that Pound's *influence* has been responsible for much of Eliot's best work.

The first of the new poems was " The Hippopotamus," written in 1917. I have made further reference to this in a later chapter, but here may be noted its debt to Gautier, by comparing its first stanza with that of the French " L'Hippopotame":

" L'Hippopotame au large ventre
    Habite aux jungles de Java ;
    Où grondent, au fond de chaque antre,
    Plus de monstres qu'on n'en rêva."

" The broad-backed hippopotamus
Rests on his belly in the mud ;
Although he seems so firm to us
He is merely flesh and blood."

In the same way the " Grishkin is nice " of
" Whispers of Immortality " has affinities with
Gautier's " Carmen est maigre," but it would
be as unprofitable to trace in detail Gautier's
influence as Laforgue's. Both it and echoes of
Donne and the Metaphysicals are sufficiently
apparent to the readers who can recognise them
and irrelevant to those who cannot. The important thing is the poem, not the references ;
not the original substances, but the new thing
which they have combined to form in the
presence of the catalyst.

   The satirical poems of 1917 and 1918 are,
" The Hippopotamus," " Whispers of Im-
mortality," " Mr. Eliot's Sunday Morning
Service," " Sweeney Erect," " Sweeney among
the Nightingales," " A Cooking Egg " and
" Burbank with a Baedeker : Bleistein with a
Cigar." As all are written in strict quatrains,
the form alone demands a maximum compression

involving more elliptical transitions, more
frequent allusions, more careful choice of words
than was necessary in the earlier work. Leisure—
even what there was of it—is lost. The verses
are concentrated to the highest possible degree,
matching the irony which is behind them. And,
as in the best Elizabethans, " the idea and the
simile become one." The concreteness of the
imagery is increased. The method—effective
enough, certainly—of :

> " Regard that woman
> Who hesitates toward you in the light of the door
> Which opens on her like a grin,"

in " Rhapsody on a Windy Night," has given
place to :

> " Rachel *née* Rabinovitch
> Tears at the grapes with murderous paws "

in " Sweeney among the Nightingales " ; and
the tentative plagiarism in " Cousin Nancy "—
" the army of unalterable law "—has become
the deliberate borrowings from at least ten
different works in " Burbank with a Baedeker :
Bleistein with a Cigar." The quotations here,

however, from "The Merchant of Venice" and "Othello : The Moor of Venice," from Ruskin's "Stones of Venice" and Browning's "A Toccata of Galuppi's" (whose scene is Venice), have the effect of creating in the reader's mind an immeasurably more detailed picture of the city which is the background of the poem than could the poem itself without the references. This, indeed, is the justification of the method. Eliot has called in the past to redress the balance of the present, using it for expansion as well as contrast.

As we see the unworthy daughter of Venice, Princess Volupine, discarding the sentimental American tourist, Burbank, in favour of the wealthy Jew, Sir Ferdinand Klein, we sense also the gradual decline of Venice, sapped by the Jew of whom Shylock was the symbol three hundred years ago and who, to-day, is represented most truly not by the respectable Klein, but by the vulgar Bleistein :

> " But this or such was Bleistein's way :
> A saggy bending of the knees
> And elbows, with the palms turned out,
> Chicago Semite Viennese.

A lustreless protrusive eye
  Stares from the protozoic slime
At a perspective of Canaletto.
  The smoky candle end of time

Declines. On the Rialto once.
  The rats are underneath the piles.
The jew is underneath the lot.
  Money in furs. The boatman smiles."

The suggestion of the past by quotation (aided by the pictorial "perspective of Canaletto") not only gives the poem a general as well as a particular application, but it also enforces the contrast between past and present in the way we have already noticed in the earlier juxta-position of La Rochefoucauld and the "Boston Evening Transcript."

This device distinguishes all the satirical poems. They are notable, too, for the poet's hatred of vulgarity, apparent in the portrait of Bleistein which kindles to white-heat in the drawing of "Apeneck Sweeney," symbol of the modern vulgarian. And on one plane of technical experiment their use of little-known words enriches the vocabulary of poetry. Though some of Eliot's followers have carried this mannerism to the point of a mania, none has succeeded in equalling his own discovery of a word which serves for the complete line—"polyphiloprogenitive."

Side by side with these English poems formed with French precision, Eliot was writing French poems in free verse—"Le Directeur," "Mélange adultère de tout," "Lune de Miel" and "Dans le Restaurant." Then, in 1919 he combined his various methods to give us what is surely one of the greatest short poems in the language, "Gerontion." Here, in the thoughts of

"an old man in a dry month
Being read to by a boy, waiting for rain,"

his mastery of his instrument is apparent, his past achievement is epitomised and the future suggested. We are on the road to "The Waste Land."

VI

" The Waste Land "

§ 1. *The Scope of the Poem*

THE publication of " The Waste Land " in
1922 marked the emergence of T. S. Eliot
as a major poet. There was of course no general
recognition of the fact ; the critics, finding that
the poem was in the nature of an enigma, were
uncertain whether or not it was merely a joke ;
Eliot's admirers, though staunch, were slightly
puzzled, but made up in enthusiasm what they
lacked in understanding, while his detractors
triumphed in its chaotic unintelligibility. If
the new technique led to this sort of thing, it
stood as poetry self-condemned ; even to-day
many readers have difficulty in appreciating fully
this short work (it contains only four hundred
and thirty-three lines), with its fifty annotated
references and other incidental allusions, its

quotations in five different languages (including Sanskrit), its elliptical phrasing and its subtle rhythms. Nor has elucidation been achieved by the efforts of several well-intentioned expositors too intent on simplifying their own explanations to trouble themselves to appreciate the full range and complexity of their subject. Even the only critic to show any real understanding of it, Mr. F. R. Leavis, is so concerned not to insult his reader's intelligence by " explaining the obvious " that he has frequently omitted to explain the recondite. For what is obvious to a scholar long familiar with " The Waste Land " may be a tiresome obscurity to the Plain Reader approaching it for the first time. Pedantry is the danger of any commentary, but here the risk of it seems the less disastrous alternative, and to any whose intelligences are insulted in the course of this chapter apologies are offered in advance.

To " explain " a poem in the sense that one explains a problem is obviously impossible. That is the main difference between art and science. The enthusiastic admirer who asked Pavlova what one of her dances meant was answered : "If I could have said it, do you suppose I should have danced it?" And certainly if Eliot had intended "The Waste Land" as an anthropological treatise or as a religious tract, he would have written it so. The main fact about "The Waste Land," never to be lost sight of, is that it is a poem. The first reading should be made without any reference to the notes at all ; without even any concern as to the "meaning." Preferably it should be read aloud, for thus are best revealed the full surge of its rhythms, the dramatic quality of its construction and the intricacy of its word texture. Like all genuine poetry, "it can communicate before it is understood."

Nor in places is understanding itself difficult—understanding at least of some part of its significance :

> " After the torchlight red on sweaty faces
> After the frosty silence in the gardens
> After the agony in stony places
> The shouting and the crying

Prison and palace and reverberation
Of thunder of spring over distant mountains
He who was living is now dead
We who were living are now dying
With a little patience."

Gethsemane, the Judgment Hall, Calvary and the rending of the rocks at the ninth hour are immediately apparent. But because there is much more in it than this, because of the wealth of allusive comment, " explanation "—once the nature of its subordinate function is realised— becomes valid.

" The Waste Land " is a poetic cryptogram. The incantatory value of the poetry is not nullified by ignorance of the " solution," though knowledge of that too is necessary for complete enjoyment. Or it might be compared with one of those Upanishads to which it refers, where the fine formal shading conceals an esoteric message. The best analogy however is that suggested by Mr. I. A. Richards when he calls Eliot's poetry a " music of ideas." " The ideas are of all kinds, abstract and concrete, general and particular and, like the musician's phrases, they are

F

arranged, not that they may tell us something, but that their effects in us may combine into a coherent whole of feeling and attitude and produce a peculiar liberation of the will.'' This method, which we have already seen at work in minor compositions, produces in " The Waste Land " a major symphony, and the " programme " of it is our civilisation.

This attempt to epitomise in a single work of art a sensitive man's reaction to the whole of experience, though made in no other age, was almost inevitable in ours. The growth of psychology has deepened our introspection at the same time as the rapid progress of other sciences has made us increasingly hopeless of assimilating a fraction of the available knowledge of the external world. We are all specialists now and our subject is ourselves. We have forsworn an objective interest in things in order to consider our subjective reaction to them.

There are two ways in which this gigantic task has been approached. One is by expansion, the other by compression. The former was adopted

by James Joyce when he took more than seven
hundred large pages to describe twenty-four hours
in a man's life ; the latter by T. S. Eliot when he
took less than five hundred lines to evoke a pano-
rama of civilisation from the earliest times till the
present day. These are perhaps the extreme limits
—though once the efficacy of the descriptive
method is admitted, it is difficult to see where
it will stop ; logically we might demand six
volumes to describe six minutes. But on the
side of compression, it is doubtful whether
"The Waste Land" can be surpassed, without
the art-form becoming merely an arid formula.

The scope of its evocations may be indicated
by saying that, on the literary side alone, it
assumes that the reader—that is, the average
educated man of sensibility—is acquainted with
the Greek myths, Virgil and Ovid, the Old and
New Testaments, the Pervigilium Veneris, St.
Augustine's "Confessions," the songs of the
Troubadours, Dante, Shakespeare and his contemporaries, the English "Metaphysicals,"
Milton, Goldsmith, Wagner, Baudelaire, Verlaine

and the French " Symbolists," and moreover
that his familiarity with them is such that they
have become part of his consciousness of experience. It is a formidable list, but even
those critics who complain of the " erudition "
implied must at least admit the catholicity and
correctness of the taste. Nor, considering the
background of the short " Burbank," for
instance, will it seem excessive to those familiar
with Eliot's method.

Yet the literary associations in " The Waste
Land " are valuable chiefly as reminders of
stages of culture and belief. In the same way
Eliot's familiar technique of contrasts is put to
more subtle uses. The contrast in " The
Waste Land " is much more than an ironic comment. It is used to suggest that apparent con-
traries are really identical. For instance in the
transition, in the third section, from the drab
love-making of the typist and the carbuncular
young man,

> " One of the low on whom assurance sits
> As a silk hat on a Bradford millionaire,"

to the badinage of Queen Elizabeth and the Earl
of Leicester on the poop of the Royal Barge,
magnificent in red and gold, the point is not the
difference, but the similarity. "All the women
are one woman," and the nostalgia for past
splendour is suddenly checked by the realisation
that it is the same as present squalor.

This simultaneity of impression, which is
the essence of "The Waste Land," accounts in
part for its "difficulty." Just as any single
thought of any one of us contains a multitude
of conflicting associations and impressions, so
every line of the poem implies several co-existing
awarenesses. The "action"—though such a
term is not strictly applicable—lies in the wilderness of mediæval legend, yet this does not prevent
it lying equally in post-War London and against
many other rapidly shifting scenes. The "spectator of the action" is Tiresias, the seer of
Greek myth, who has "foresuffered all," who
knows all events from the beginning to the end
of time, and who has experienced life both as a
man and as a woman. It is this character, the

personification of an abstract all-embracing human consciousness, which gives the poem its unity. The reader, losing his own identity, sees contemporary civilisation through Tiresias's eyes.

In this civilisation he finds that sex has ceased to be a sacrament and has become an obsession. No longer is the great rhythm of Nature—birth, mating and death—obeyed by men in cities. Ours is an age of *affaires*. Yet without mating the circle is shattered ; it becomes a line ending in nothingness—birth death—instead of the un-ending cycle—birth mating death birth mating death birth . . . Without mating the old, dying, cannot be reborn in the young. There is no resurrection.

So the age has lost its potency, and we, its children, have betrayed our trust. And it is imperative that the power be regained, the treason atoned. For this, one thing alone will suffice—a period of ascetic renunciation. By using the flesh in a selfish, shallow manner we have thwarted life ; to restore life by abstinence must be our penance. To see in '' The Waste Land '' merely a lamentable picture of disintegration is to miss the entire point of it. That picture indeed Eliot has painted, and painted superbly. But there is also a cry from the wilderness, a call to repentance. It reminds us that without renouncement there is no rebirth, and that there is a point where purity becomes synonymous with chastity. To find in it a dry, sub-human revulsion against love, or a defeatist fear of life (which nearly every writer on Eliot has affected to discover there), is to misread it still more completely. Love is never mentioned ; there is only the destructive, sterile passion of an Isolde or a Cleopatra, the spineless weakness of an Ophelia, the lewd vanity of a Bianca, the neurasthenic flirtation of a *grande dame*, the ignorant vulgarity of a typist, the exhausted vitality of a slum dweller. It was the "love" (if you define the word thus) of Guinevere which brought about the disruption of the ordered, creative chivalry of the Round Table. Not to Lancelot, but to Galahad and Parsifal, is revealed the secret of the life-giving Grail.

§ 2. *The Title and its Meaning*

" Not only the title, but the plan and a good deal of the incidental symbolism of the poem were suggested by Miss Jessie L. Weston's book on the Grail Legend : ' From Ritual to Romance.' Indeed, so deeply am I indebted, Miss Weston's book will elucidate the difficulties of the poem much better than my notes can do ; and I recommend it (apart from the great interest of the book itself) to any who think such elucidation of the poem worth the trouble." Thus Eliot in his introductory note ; and a reading of the book certainly solves many of the obscurities. But as not every reader may have access to it (it is now unfortunately out of print), a résumé of its thesis may not be superfluous.

Miss Weston has shown that the famous romance of the Grail Quest has its origin in the most primitive of all cults—the Fertility Ritual. It was instituted in an age of " sympathetic magic " by our Aryan forefathers (parallels

to the Grail legend occur in the Rig-Veda
hymns), and can be traced through the cults of
Tammuz and Adonis and the mystery religions
of the Roman Empire, to reappear, modified by
Christianity, in the songs of the Troubadours
in twelfth-century Europe.   On these the famous
romancers like Malory worked, not realising
always the nature of the material with which
they were dealing, until the age of chivalry died
and, with it, it too vanished.   Then, in the
century of the Industrial Revolution, it was
suddenly rediscovered by poets, musicians and
painters, and the genius of Tennyson and his
contemporaries, of Wagner, of the Pre-Raphaelites
restored it once more to the consciousness of
men.   But by this time the original significance
of the stories was altogether lost, nor was
their progress from ritual to romance even
understood.

Whether this explanation be accepted in its
entirety or not, its correctness must be assumed
for the purposes of the poem, for Eliot has
assumed it, and it alone gives meaning to many

of the references to India, Egypt, Phœnicia, Greece and Rome.

The essence of the legend (though details vary in different versions) is of how the Questing Knight saved the Waste Land. The old age and infirmity of its ruler, who is known as the Fisher King, entail dire consequences on the land itself. It languishes under a prolonged drought which has destroyed all life and vegetation. The hero must restore to the King his youth and health, which change, by "sympathetic" reaction on his kingdom, will "free the waters" and bring back fertility to the country. For this it is necessary for the Pure Knight to ride to the Perilous Chapel and there question of the Lance and the Grail, ancient symbols of the male and female principles of life. His failure to question will mean continued drought and disaster ; his success, the salvation of King and land.

§ 3. " The Burial of the Dead "

In a waste land the greatest agony is at the time of the resurrection of the year, when, surrounded

by its sterility, one can see the spring only in
memory. So the poem opens :

> '' April is the cruellest month, breeding
> Lilacs out of the dead land, mixing
> Memory and desire, stirring
> Dull roots with spring rain.
> Winter kept us warm, covering
> Earth in forgetful snow, feeding
> A little life with dried tubers.''

In the next sentence we are in Central Europe,
among a crowd of gossiping, cosmopolitan
idlers, and the waste land of to-day reveals itself
by a few disjointed scraps of conversation.
The two are fused in a fine rhetorical passage,
where old age and infirmity are suggested, not
by a reference to the Fisher King, but by a hint of
the wonderful closing section of Ecclesiastes,
with its description of the days '' when they shall
be afraid of that which is high, and fears shall
be in the way, and the almond tree shall
flourish, and the grasshopper shall be a burden,
and desire shall fail.'' The atmosphere created
by this introduction of the Old Testament is
reinforced by the reminiscence of the prophesied

time when "a man shall be as the shadow of a
great rock in a weary land." And the appellation
"Son of man," with its inevitable association
with the Crucified One, suggests the connection
—to become more apparent later—between Jesus
and the slain Vegetation God :

> " What are the roots that clutch, what branches grow
>   Out of this stony rubbish ?   Son of man,
>   You cannot say, or guess, for you know only
>   A heap of broken images, where the sun beats,
>   And the dead tree gives no shelter, the cricket no
>   relief,
>   And the dry stone no sound of water.   Only
>   There is shadow under this red rock,
>   (Come in under the shadow of this red rock),
>   And I will show you something different from
>   either
>   Your shadow at morning striding behind you
>   Or your shadow at evening rising to meet you ;
>   I will show you fear in a handful of dust."

Suddenly the key changes. Four lines of the
sailor lad's song, at the opening of Wagner's
"Tristan und Isolde," as the ship bears the
lovers to Ireland, recall another legend of
romance, in spirit far removed from the Grail
story—one where an unlawful passion brings

treachery and death in its train. But at the
moment the love-potion is still untasted ; Tristan
still stands glooming apart ; there is still hope.
We are not allowed to forget the ending of it,
however. Eight lines later another phrase is
recalled. This time it is from the last act,
when the dying Tristan, far now from Ireland,
having broken his faith and himself having been
broken by passion, asks in vain whether Isolde's
ship is on the horizon, to receive answer :

> " *Od' und leer das Meer.*"
> ("Waste and empty is the sea.")

Between these two quotations comes a personal
note, a memory, a confession "that desire has
failed " :

> " You gave me hyacinths first a year ago ;
> ' They called me the hyacinth girl.'
> —Yet when we came back, late, from the Hyacinth
>   garden,
> Your arms full, and your hair wet, I could not
> Speak, and my eyes failed, I was neither
> Living nor dead, and I knew nothing,
> Looking into the heart of light, the silence."

This memory is associated with the reminiscences

of childhood in the earlier conversation in the Hofgarten. The connecting link is to be found in Eliot's own French poem, "Dans le Restaurant," in which the old waiter babbles of a childish love-scene and laughter and a gift of cowslips in the rain. It is, too, the symbolic memory which haunts the earlier poems, especially "La Figlia che Piange" and "Portrait of a Lady." "Dans le Restaurant," however, is the real key, for its relationship to "The Waste Land" is unmistakable by reason of the fact that its last seven lines, translated and adapted, form the fourth section of this poem.

The symbolism of the hyacinth, flower of the spring—a flower too associated, like the lilac, with the Slain God—reinforces the significance of the sea, the element from which all life sprang. The echoing of water in the whole passage is itself dramatic enough after the dry misery and fear of the previous section, and there are few better examples of Eliot's genius for quotation than the single line lamenting that the very sea is waste.

The next seventeen lines describe a fashionable clairvoyante, Madame Sosostris, fortune-telling by means of a pack of Tarot cards. Their first and immediate effect is to emphasise the futile inanity of the sophisticated society which we have already met prattling in Münich, by the reminder that the majestic figure of Tiresias has shrunk to the sniffling Sosostris "known to be the wisest woman in Europe" with her

> "Thank you. If you see dear Mrs. Equitone,
> Tell her I bring the horoscope myself;
> One must be so careful these days."

Yet in so far as she represents in some sort the "spectator of the action," she introduces some of the "characters" of the drama—the figures in the Tarot pack which the poet has either chosen or invented to suit his purpose.

There is the drowned Phœnician Sailor, brought over from "Dans le Restaurant," whom a quotation from "The Tempest" connects with Ferdinand, Prince of Naples, and who in another aspect becomes the twentieth-century

> "Mr. Eugenides, the Smyrna merchant,
> Unshaven, with a pocketful of currants."

There is " Belladonna, the Lady of the Rocks, the lady of situations," the woman who is all women and whose nature is sufficiently indicated by her title. There is the Man with Three Staves, who is associated "quite arbitrarily with the Fisher King himself." There is the Wheel—the eternal cycle. But at present the Hanged Man is not there—the Hanged Man who stands both for the Slain God and the Hooded Figure on the road to Emmaus in the last section of the poem. There is no redemption, only more signs of futility and despair—the despair of "Fear death by water," the life-giver, and the futility of "crowds of people walking round in a ring," the mob which appears again and again as a kind of macabre chorus ; now the crowd of apathetic English workers flowing over London Bridge, now the Russian proletariat regimented and menacing, "endless hordes" awaiting hungrily the collapse of the European culture ; now the "sweaty faces" at the great betrayal in Gethsemane, and now the "red sullen faces" of the dwellers in the Waste Land who

" sneer and snarl
From doors of mudcracked houses."

Here at least is a change which is easily seen as a
constant.   The mob never alters.

The use of the Tarot pack is not fortuitous.
The origin of these cards, the ancestors of the
present playing-cards, is not certainly known,
but, to quote Miss Weston, " what is certain is
that these cards are used to-day by the Gipsies
for purposes of divination." What is equally
certain and more to the point is that they form
another channel through which the underlying
meaning of the Grail Quest has reached us—
another repository of the secrets of the ancient
ritual.   The four suits, corresponding to Hearts,
Diamonds, Spades and Clubs, are Cup, Lance,
Sword and Dish.   This alone is sufficiently
suggestive for, in the words of Mr. W. B. Yeats,
" Cup, Lance, Dish, Sword, in slightly varying
forms, have never lost their mystic significance."
They are found in a calendar of the twenty-third
dynasty of Egypt, which " is supposed to have
been connected with the periodic rise and fall of

G

the waters of the Nile '' ; the names of some
of the figures can be traced to a Sanskrit source ;
and even in China the Tarot has been discovered
on a monument '' traditionally erected in com-
memoration of the drying up of the waters of the
Deluge.''

These associations give sufficient force to the
line referring to '' a wicked pack of cards.''

We are now in London :

'' Unreal City,
    Under the brown fog of a winter dawn,
    A crowd flowed over London Bridge, so many,
    I had not thought death had undone so many.
    Sighs, short and infrequent, were exhaled,
    And each man fixed his eyes before his feet.
    Flowed up the hill and down King William Street,
    To where Saint Mary Woolnoth kept the hours
    With a dead sound on the final stroke of nine.''

The descriptive force of this passage, considered
without any of its implications, is striking
enough. The Waste Land has extended its
boundaries to embrace the capital city of civilisation. But the under-current connects it with
two other cities as well—with Baudelaire's

" Fourmillante, cité, cité pleine de rêves,
   Où le spectre en plein jour raccroche le passant,"

and with Dante's " Inferno."

" I had not thought death had undone so many," says Dante, standing just within the portal of Hell and seeing the vast crowd of spirits who rush confusedly round a wavering flag. These spirits, as Virgil explains to him, are those who " lived without praise or blame, who did nothing strongly nor believed in anything but themselves." Even Death refuses them, and they must for ever keep in aimless, fevered motion. " Their blind life passes so meanly that they envy all other lots ; both mercy and justice scorn them." For " Heaven chased them forth to keep its beauty from impair, and deep Hell receives them not, because the wicked would have some glory over them."

Never perhaps has the mob been so accurately defined, and the vision recurs again in Eliot's work when in a critical essay he writes : " So far as we are human, what we do must be either evil or good ; so far as we do evil or good, we are human ; and it is better, in a paradoxical way, to do evil than to do nothing ; at least we exist. It is true to say that the glory of man is his capacity for salvation ; it is equally true to say that his glory is his capacity for damnation. The worst that can be said for most of our malefactors, from statesmen to thieves, is that they are not men enough to be damned.'' And again, the same thought and the same Dante passage determines Eliot's next poem, '' The Hollow Men.''

The doom of Laodicea is not the least of the horrors of the Waste Land.

'' I had not thought death had undone so many.''

In the next line :

'' Sighs, short and infrequent, were exhaled,''

we follow Dante into Limbo, where are the sighing spirits who desire God, but having died before the revelation in Christ, and having lived in a waste land before the ''freeing of the waters,'' having known no Resurrection, now '' without hope live in desire.''

The church of Saint Mary Woolnoth, which
" kept the hours," is related (by the repetition of
that phrase in the last section) to the Perilous
Chapel ; and the menace of the " dead sound
on the stroke of nine " (a purely personal
observation) suggests the hallucinatory atmosphere
which traditionally surrounds that goal of the
Quest. From this point the " unreal city "
passes into the feverish inconsequence of a nightmare, in the eight lines which bring the first
section of the poem to a close :

" There I saw one I knew, and stopped him, crying :
   ' Stetson.
  ' You who were with me in the ships at Mylæ !
  That corpse you planted last year in your garden,
  Has it begun to sprout ? Will it bloom this year ?
  Or has the sudden frost disturbed its bed ?
  Oh keep the Dog far hence, that's friend to men,
  Or with his nails he'll dig it up again !
  You ! hypocrite lecteur !—mon semblable—mon
   frère ! ' "

The divination of dreams is both difficult and
dangerous, and an *analysis* of this passage is
practically impossible. It is too intentionally
disorganised. It is true that endings of the third

and the fifth sections of the poem are in certain respects similar in point of compression and richness of association, but whereas, in the third, the use of simple phrases evokes enormous backgrounds (as the enunciation of a theme may suggest entire symphony), and in the fifth, the crowd of quotations serves as a kind of coda to the whole poem, in this there is all the inconsequence of a rebellious rhapsody. It is only possible therefore to note certain *motifs* whose presence relates it to the rest of the work.

The most important reference is to the title, " The Burial of the Dead." In some versions of the Grail story it is the death of a King or Knight which causes the plight of the Fisher King and his land, while, in the myths and the mysteries, the slaying of the God and his burial are of course the necessary preludes to resurrection. The hopeless days are those between Good Friday and Easter.

In "Mylæ," a sea-battle in which the Carthaginians were defeated, comes the second of those references to the Phœnicians or to their city of

Carthage, which recur in one form or another until Phlebas, the Phœnician Sailor, meets his death by water. At first glance it is difficult to see the relevance of the introduction of the Phœnicians except as another civilisation to add to the world-conspectus. But when it is realised that the worship of Adonis originated in Phœnicia, and that in his person the earlier Sumerian-Babylonian Tammuz, heir to the Aryan Vegetation Gods, entered the Western world, Carthage acquires a new importance.

In his note on the lines :

" ' Oh keep the Dog far hence, that's friend to men,
    Or with his nails he'll dig it up again ! ' "

Eliot refers us to the source of the allusion— the Dirge in Webster's " The White Devil," which runs :

" Call for the robin-redbreast and the wren
    Since o'er shady groves they hover,
    And with leaves and flowers do cover
    The friendless bodies of unburied men.
    Call unto his funeral dole
    The ant, the field-mouse, and the mole,

To rear him hillocks that shall keep him warm,
And (when gay tombs are robbed) sustain no harm.
But keep the wolf far thence, that's foe to men,
For with his nails he'll dig them up again."

But not only is Webster's song to the point, but
also Charles Lamb's comment on it : " I never
saw anything like this dirge, except the ditty
which reminds Ferdinand of his drowned father
in the 'Tempest.' As that is of the water,
watery, so this is of the earth, earthy.''

The " Dog " of course is Sirius, the Dog Star,
which in Egypt was regarded as the herald of the
fertilising floods of the Nile. Its appearance,
foretelling the rising of the waters, marked the
Egyptian New Year, the feast of Isis, whose tears,
they said, swelled the river in mourning for
her slain husband, Osiris (the equivalent of the
Phœnician-Greek Adonis).

Then dramatically the section ends with a
line from Baudelaire, which turns suddenly
on the reader, reminding him that he too, for all
his complacent detachment, is involved in the
stupidity, sin and indecency of a world which is a
waste land.

§ 4. II—*A Game of Chess*

The second section of the poem, ‘‘A Game
of Chess,’’ is (if we except the short ‘‘Phlebas
the Phœnician ’’) the most easily understood.
It has obvious unity of idea and symmetry of
form. The narrative passages, the dialogue and
the transition from splendour to squalor present
no difficulties. Nor does the inevitable contrast
obscure similarity. Even without the knowledge
that the various women are one, the reader could
sense the identification of the woman in the
palace whose luxury is suggested by :

‘‘ In vials of ivory and coloured glass
    Unstoppered, lurked her strange synthetic perfumes,
    Unguent, powdered, or liquid—troubled, confused
    And drowned the sense in odours ; ’’

with the woman in the public-house and her
delighted memory :

‘‘ Well, that Sunday Albert was home, they had a
        hot gammon,
    And they asked me in to dinner, to get the beauty
        of it hot——’’

Technically, too, the section is, in a way, self-

contained. It affords an admirable illustration
of the range of modern poetry in general and
Eliot's verse in particular. The first part
beats the Romantics on their own ground
(Laura Riding and Robert Graves in their
" Survey of Modernist Poetry " have pointed
out how pale a parallel passage from Keats
appears beside it) : the second part exposes
any pre-War attempts at " realism " for the
shoddy " poetic " affectations that they are.
And, this cohesion apart, its place in the logical
development of the poem's central idea is not
obscure. After the burial of the dead comes the
refusal of life—the sterility which denies resurrection—

> " What you get married for if you don't want
>   children ? "

Woman, the mother of all living, is only " Belladonna, the Lady of the Rocks, the lady of
situations."

The opening lines :

> " The chair she sat in, like a burnished throne
> Glowed on the marble,"

directly connect her with Cleopatra, as Eno-
barbus describes :

> " The barge she sat in, like a burnished throne,
> Burned on the waters."

The adaptation becomes a comment on the echo.
There is no water here ; only the sense is
drowned in odours and

> " Huge sea-wood fed with copper
> Burned green and orange, framed by the coloured
>   stone,
> In which sad light a carved dolphin swam."

And the reminiscence of Cleopatra brings to
mind " the great whore that sitteth upon many
waters," the woman of Revelation, " arrayed
in purple and scarlet colour and decked with gold
and precious stones," an association enforced by

> " —the flames of seven-branched candelabra
> Reflecting light upon the table as
> The glitter of her jewels rose to meet it."

Then a few lines further, a mention of " the
laquearia" recalls the Æneid and the story of the
passion of Dido, Queen of Carthage.

There is no relief from this stifling interior ;

even " the air that freshened from the window "
seems heavy and polluted. And what little
escape there is is pregnant with doom.   For

> " Above the antique mantel was displayed
> As though a window gave upon the sylvan scene
> The change of Philomel, by the barbarous king
> So rudely forced ; yet there is the nightingale
> Filled all the desert with inviolable voice
> And still she cried, and still the world pursues,
> ' Jug Jug ' to dirty ears."

Without the help of the author's note, even
fewer readers would connect the two words
" sylvan scene " with a passage from " Paradise
Lost " than would have found the Æneid in
" laquearia." Nor, it might seem, would
the lack of it be so great a loss here as in many
other instances. For is there not a sufficient
dramatic force in the mere juxtaposition of the
fresh air of the country-side with the heavy
languor of the room?

The presence of the note, however, reminds us
again (if we had forgotten it) that Eliot's poetic
method is not concerned to make loose romantic
generalisations which each reader will interpret

in terms of his own individual experience, but
to particularise a definite image. The " sylvan
scene " is not to inspire a flight of our own fancy
to lush meadows containing old unhappy bulls
but to direct our thoughts to Satan viewing
from the borders of Eden the distant prospect
of Paradise which crowns

> " —the champaign head
> Of a steep wilderness, whose hairy sides
> With thicket overgrown, grotesque and wild,
> Access denied : and overhead up grew
> Insuperable height of loftiest shade,
> Cedar, and pine, and fir, and branching palm,
> A sylvan scene."

The fact that there is something menacing in the
aspect prepares the way for the grim Greek legend
that follows. (Incidentally the juxtaposition
of the two mythologies becomes more interesting
in view of Eliot's *mot* elsewhere that "Milton's
celestial and infernal regions are large but
insufficiently furnished apartments filled by heavy
conversation ; and one remarks about the
Puritan mythology an historical thinness.")

The waste land on the slopes of Paradise

changes to the waste land of Heleas in whose
solitudes Tereus, King of Thrace, having forced
Philomela to his will, cut out her tongue that
she might not tell her sister Procne of the out-
rage.   But Procne discovered the truth and terrible
was her revenge.   She served as a meal to Tereus,
her husband, the murdered body of their son.
The very barbarity of this myth sharpens its
appropriateness to the theme of " The Waste
Land," and references to it and to the sequel
—the metamorphosis of Philomela into a
nightingale so that the withered stump of her
tongue became an " inviolable voice," and of
Procne into a swallow—are to appear again.

The room now has become more sinister than
ever.

> " And other withered stumps of time
> Were told upon the walls ; staring forms
> Leaned out, leaning, hushing the room enclosed.
> Footsteps shuffled on the stair."

Against this background starts the neurasthenic
conversation of the woman, answered by the
thoughts of the man :

" ' My nerves are bad to-night. Yes, bad. Stay
    with me.
Speak to me. Why do you never speak. Speak.
What are you thinking of? What thinking?
    What?
I never know what you are thinking. Think.'
" ' I think we are in rats' alley,
Where the dead men lost their bones.'
' What is that noise? '
            The wind under the door.
' What is that noise now? What is the wind
    doing?'
            Nothing again nothing."

The wind recalling the horrors of Webster's
plays by the line " Is the wind in that door still? "
—one of the few memorable moments in " The
Devil's Law Case "—increases the macabre
tension as the conversation continues :

            " ' Do
You know nothing? Do you see nothing? Do you
    remember
Nothing?'
            I remember
Those are pearls that were his eyes.
' Are you alive, or not? Is there nothing in your
    head?'"

The repetitions of " nothing " increase the

Websterian atmosphere, echoing the famous conversation in " The Duchess of Malfi " between Flamineo and his murderer, while " The Tempest " passage, recurring again, in these surroundings suggests that Shakespeare himself has undergone a sea-change. In the melancholy of the man's thoughts there is a certain stoic dignity ; now they become vehement in revolt against the vacuous vulgarity of it all. There is nothing

> " But
> O O O O that Shakespeherian Rag—
> It's so elegant
> So intelligent
> ' What shall I do now ? What shall I do ?
> I shall rush out as I am, and walk the street
> With my hair down, so. What shall we do to-
> morrow ?
> What shall we ever do ? '
> The hot water at ten.
> And if it rains, a closed car at four.
> And we shall play a game of chess,
> Pressing lidless eyes and waiting for a knock upon
> the door."

The game of chess, which also gives the section its title, recalls the most superb example of

dramatic irony in the whole range of English
literature, that scene in Middleton's " Women
Beware Women " when Bianca meets the Duke.
Her old mother-in-law, unsuspecting, has come
to play chess with her neighbour Livia in whose
house the Duke is concealed. While the game is
in progress, Bianca is taken over the house to see
its treasures and finally comes upon the last and
greatest, hidden behind an arras—the Duke
himself. The staging is so contrived that the
audience sees on the upper stage the meeting
between the two and hears the Duke's passionate
avowal of his love, while on the fore-stage below
the game continues its placid way. This appeal
to the eye emphasises tenfold the verbal irony of
such a passage as Livia's

" Did I not say my duke would fetch you o'er,
  Widow?
  I think you spoke in earnest when you said it,
  madam.
  And my black King makes all the haste he can too.
  Well, madam, we may meet with him in time yet.
  I've given thee blind mate twice."

So there is still another woman added to the
H

gallery, Bianca, who, in Eliot's words is "as real as any woman in Elizabethan tragedy, the type of woman who is purely moved by vanity." The betrayal of love is at the hands of a woman.

The game of chess, itself a sober enough pastime, has acquired a new meaning, and another still is added by the suggestion of death in the "knock upon the door." Now it is symbolical of the unfruitful waste of time which is the lot of purposeless existence. "The real tragedy of life is that nothing happens and that the resulting monotony does not kill."

The knock itself is used for the transition to the next scene. It becomes the repeated "HURRY UP PLEASE ITS TIME" of the barman at closing time, breaking through the gossip of the women in the public-house. At first a friendly warning, it announces that ten o'clock has indubitably struck at the close. After a double repetition of it farewells are hiccupped on the pavement :

"Goonight Bill. Goonight Lou. Goonight May. Goonight. Ta ta. Goonight. Goonight.'

and the last line :

" Good night, ladies, good night, sweet ladies, good
night, good night,"

transports us to another place where deep drink-
ing was a custom and at the Court of Denmark
we catch a momentary glimpse of her, " of all
ladies most deject and wretched," Ophelia,
whose failure in loyalty to Hamlet at the critical
moment in his life spelt death and ruin for so
many.

§ 5. III—*The Fire Sermon*

Much of the third movement is in the nature
of recapitulation, re-stating the themes, while
at the same time it develops them, investing
them with an added richness, and leads up to a
magnificent climax. The orchestration is more
subtle, more brilliantly surprising here than any-
where else in the poem. If the section lacks the
excitement of novelty which distinguishes the
first, the simplicity of design of the second and
the soaring grandeur of the fifth, its masterly
craftsmanship is ample compensation.

The title, as in " The Burial of the Dead "

and " A Game of Chess," is not immediately explained ; here, indeed, it indicates the climax rather than the general content and is hidden till three lines before the end. Only on the second reading do we realise the full import of it. Then we are transported to Gaya Head, where to the thousand priests Buddha is delivering that discourse on fire during which the minds of his hearers " became free from attachment and delivered from depravities." The substance of the sermon is that all things are burning—sight and sound and taste and smell, imagination and consciousness, and all sensations which reach the soul through these channels. " And with what are these burning? With the fire of passion, say I, with the fire of hatred, with the fire of infatuation, with birth, old age, death, sorrow, lamentation, misery, grief and despair are they burning."

The learned and noble disciple, perceiving this, conceives an aversion for these channels of fire, " and in conceiving this aversion, he becomes divested of passion, and by the absence of passion he becomes free, and when he is free he becomes aware that he is free and he knows that re-birth is exhausted, that he has lived the holy life, that he has done what it behoved him to do and that he is no more for this world."

Fire, as a symbol, has a double significance. It is both the destroyer and the purifier ; but here it is conceived only in its first aspect—as the antithesis of the life-giving element of water. The threefold fire of the Buddhists is the three-fold fever of life—lust (greed), hatred and in-fatuation. The analogy is not " gold tried in the fire," but " a brand plucked from the burning." The mistake is often made of assign-ing a constant meaning to the symbol and seeing an invocation of the fire where there is only a warning against it. It is not until the very end of " The Waste Land " that the other, the more specifically Christian, interpretation is used and the paradox of " death by water " is completed by " salvation by fire." At present it is still author of the drought and the sterility of the parched land ; the force of " The Fire Sermon "

is to change it from a negative and secondary
cause into a positive menace, to define the
application of the allegory. By reason of the
fire, even what water there is is fruitless.

The scene, like that of " A Game of Chess,"
is modern London, with references to an
Elizabethan background of splendour :

> " The river's tent is broken : the last fingers of leaf
> Clutch and sink into the wet bank.   The wind
> Crosses the brown land, unheard.   The nymphs
>   are departed.
> Sweet Thames, run softly, till I end my song.
> The river bears no empty bottles, sandwich papers,
> Silk handkerchiefs, cardboard boxes, cigarette ends
> Or other testimony of summer nights.   The
>   nymphs are departed.
> And their friends, the loitering heirs of city
>   directors ;
> Departed, have left no addresses."

The echoes of Spenser's " Prothalamion," that
matchless " Spousal Verse " with its burden
" Sweet Thames run softly till I end my song "
and its memory of the " flock of nymphs " :

> " All lovely Daughters of the Flood thereby,
> With goodly greenish locks all loose untied,
> As each had been a Bride,"

is here used in Eliot's earlier manner of simple contrast, but Spenser's poem, once recalled, revives a memory of the now-brown land

" . . . painted with variable flowers
And all the meads adorned with dainty gems
Fit to deck maidens' bowers
And crown their paramours
Against the bridal day which is not long."

But "Sweet Thames" is only the river of exile and sorrow :

" By the waters of Leman I sat down and wept . . ."

and the air is heavy with death and decay :

" But at my back in a cold blast I hear
The rattle of the bones, and chuckle spread from
ear to ear."

The contemplation of the skull is again particularised by the reference to the passage of Marvell which is one of the peaks of " Metaphysical " poetry :

" But at my back I always hear
Time's winged chariot hurrying near :
And yonder all before us lie
Deserts of vast eternity.
Thy beauty shall no more be found :
Nor, in thy marble vault, shall sound

My echoing song : then worms shall try
That long preserv'd virginity :
And your quaint honour turn to dust ;
And into ashes all my lust.
The grave's a fine and private place,
But none I think do there embrace."

Among the complexity of associations of the
next twenty lines recur the thoughts of the man
in " A Game of Chess." Again " we are in
rats' alley where the dead men lost their bones " ;
again we see Ferdinand, Prince of Naples,

" Musing upon the king my brother's wreck
    And on the king my father's death before him " ;

again the legend of the nightingale is recalled :

" Twit twit twit
Jug jug jug jug jug jug
So rudely forc'd
Tereu."

At the outset the scene is localised and the
dreariness of it matched in words and rhythm :

" A rat crept softly through the vegetation
    Dragging its slimy belly on the bank
    While I was fishing in the dull canal
    On a winter evening round behind the gashouse."

The next two lines (already quoted), recalling

Ferdinand, Prince of Naples, immediately suggest
the obvious contrast between the sluggish canal
reflecting the monumental ugliness of the
twentieth-century gashouse, and the roar of
the sea on the beach of Prospero's enchanted
island. But more important is the association
of ideas which introduces for the first time in the
poem itself (though, of course, he has been
mentioned in the notes and his presence implied
all through "The Waste Land" by reason of
its title) the person of the Fisher King.

His central place in the legend we already
know ; it must also be remembered that his
occupation, both there and here, reinforces
the prevailing life symbolism. For the "Fish
is a Life symbol of immemorial antiquity" ;
it is found in the earliest Indian myths, and later
was transferred to the Buddha, reaching China
through the channels of Buddhism. In the
West it became a central symbol of the Orphic
mysteries, whence it was taken and adapted by
the early Christians, already familiar with it
in Judaism itself. The idea of their great

Sacramental Fish-meal, to which the Catacombs bear pictorial witness, survived into the Grail romances and explains much there that appears irrelevant, especially the connection, in some versions, between the Grail itself and a Fish. This connection is still preserved in one of the Tarot cards, the Page of Cups.

So the dull landscape with its solitary figure becomes suddenly transformed by the splendour of ages of tradition and charged with the significance of centuries. The main theme is re-stated and in the next eleven lines developed by means of new associations :

" White bodies naked on the low damp ground
    And bones cast in a little low dry garret,
    Rattled by the rat's foot only, year to year.
    But at my back from time to time I hear
    The sound of horns and motors, which shall bring
    Sweeney to Mrs. Porter in the spring.
    O the moon shone bright on Mrs. Porter
    And on her daughter
    They wash their feet in soda water
    Et O ces voix d'enfants, chantant dáns la coupole ! "

Memory of Death by water and the horror of bones in the drought are hardly disturbed by

thought of the coming spring. For still the
spring is empty. An echo of Marvell's line
again, suggesting now the continuance of death
in the season of renewal, is immediately followed
by a reminiscence of the passage from Day's
" Parliament of Bees " :

" When of a sudden, listening, you shall hear
  A noise of horns and hunting, which shall bring
  Actæon to Diana in the spring
  Where all shall see her naked skin . . ."

with the beauty of the ancient myth grotesquely
distorted into the visit of Sweeney, the modern
vulgarian in his motor-car, to the too-obvious
Mrs. Porter. A snatch of an Australian ballad
(whose import may be guessed with sufficient
ease) completes the bitterness of the transition.
But this time the contrast is instantly reversed.
From the depth of the ridiculous we pass to the
height of the sublime. Mrs. Porter's eccentricity
reminds us of another washing of feet, which
took place on the eve of a Crucifixion. The
line from Verlaine's sonnet " Parsifal " transports us to the chapel of the Grail, where during

the ceremonial washing of the feet the boy choristers in the dome remind us that :

> " The faith here lives,
> The Saviour gives
> The Dove, His dearest Token.
> Take at His board
> The Wine outpoured
> And Bread of Life here broken."

Then a snatch of the nightingale song ("'Jug jug' to dirty ears ") reintroduces the Tereus myth for a moment before we return to modern London to meet the Smyrna merchant, who is also the Phœnician sailor, for the last time.

The sudden impact of the jargon of commerce :

> " . . . currants
> C.i.f. London : documents at sight "

(which, as Eliot explains in a note, means that " the currants were quoted at a price ' carriage and insurance free to London,' and the Bill of Lading, etc., were to be handed to the buyer upon payment of the sight draft "), defines the secondary symbolism of the character. In this crazy age of mammon-worshippers, there is no god but commerce, and the banker and the economist are his prophets. Its most typical representative is the merchant ; his language its secret liturgy. Here is not the potentiality of life lost in sterile passion, but a denial of all true life-values so complete that the advent of the water can only result in its destruction. He is not even a merchant prince, and his idea of felicity, perfectly suggested in two lines, is

‘‘ . . . luncheon at the Cannon Street Hotel
Followed by a week-end at the Metropole.’’

The atmosphere of this commercial civilisation hangs heavy over the next episode. It opens

‘‘ At the violet hour, when the eyes and back
Turn upward from the desk, when the human engine waits
Like a taxi throbbing waiting . . .’’

and the hint of Sappho’s poetry side by side with the mechanical analogy sufficiently suggests the extent to which the rhythm of nature has been broken. In the agricultural community of the Ægean island, the violet hour of evening ‘‘ bringing in all that bright morning scattered ’’ was the natural time for cessation from fruitful toil ; now it is an arbitrary signal, fixed to the minute, which brings to millions of unwilling workers release from tasks as futile as they are distasteful. Nor is the life outside their work less unnatural :

> " The typist, home at tea-time, clears her breakfast, lights
> Her stove, and lays out food in tins."

Through the eyes of Tiresias we see the love affair of this lady and her admirer, the small house-agent's clerk, and the hopeless squalor of it all is pointed by another reminiscence at the end. This time Goldsmith's lines bring to mind a century which for all its coarseness at least possessed sensibility :

> " When lovely woman stoops to folly and
> Paces about her room again, alone,
> She smoothes her hair with automatic hand,
> And puts a record on the gramophone."

The memory of the eighteenth century is to the point. The formal rhyme and metre of the narrative recall the age of literary classicism just as the realism of its content gives it the quality of a Hogarth painting. And this raises an important point. Some readers have found difficulty in reconciling Eliot's hatred of and recoil from vulgarity, which is evident in the whole body of his work, with a certain coarseness apparent in this and similar passages. This is due, I think, to the failure to distinguish between the vulgar and the coarse, which vitiates so much contemporary criticism. The two are, needless to say, practically antithetical. The vulgarian is usually far too " refined " to dare to be coarse, and coarseness implies too much sensibility to admit of vulgarity. Coarseness can inspire a healthy belly-laughter, arising from the over-flow of vitality and good spirits ; vulgarity only an arid snigger at a sly innuendo. Vulgarity always implies lack of vigour. Most great works of art have moments of coarseness—the Bible and Shakespeare not excepted. But there is in them " no vile or vulgar thing." The Greeks were often coarse ; the Romans usually vulgar. To come nearer home, the deterioration of English humour from the expansive freshness of the

eighteenth century to the dry, attenuated sentimental indecency it is to-day offers an apt and
easily accessible illustration. Or, in English
painting, compare the coarseness of Hogarth
with the vulgarity of the Leighton–Poynter
school ! There is no need to pursue the comparison except to add that our recoil from
coarseness is often the measure of our vulgarity.

The vulgar noise of the typist's record provides,
by way of another reference to " The Tempest,"
the transition to a corner of London where we
can hear music at first hand, meet life in the
rough, remember an occupation which is age-
old and productive and then, as a complement—
not this time as contrast—glimpse one of the
loveliest works of art in the city which a commercial civilisation, for utilitarian reasons, is
proposing to destroy.

> " ' This music crept by me upon the waters '
> And along the Strand, up Queen Victoria Street.
> O City, city, I can sometimes hear,
> Beside a public bar in Lower Thames Street,
> The pleasant whining of a mandoline
> And a clatter and a chatter from within

Where fishmen lounge at noon : where the walls
Of Magnus Martyr hold
Inexplicable splendour of Ionian white and gold."

The fishermen direct our thoughts to the river,
no longer in its upper reaches haunted by the
nymphs, but at the Pool where

" The barges drift
  With the turning tide
  Red sails
  Wide
  To leeward, swing on the heavy spar,"

and the barge becomes the Royal Barge of Queen
Elizabeth where she rallies her favourite, Leicester,
with talk of impossible love. " They began
to talk nonsense and went so far that Lord
Robert at last said there was no reason why they
should not be married if the Queen pleased."
But Lord Robert knew, as well as the
Queen did, how nonsensical it was. It is
even more futile, though it appears more
splendid, than the *affaire* between the clerk and
the typist.

In the rhythms of these two stanzas, there is an
unmistakable echo of Wagner's " Ring." Even

I

without the note to tell us that this is the Song of the Thames Daughters, we should catch the reminiscence of the Rhine Maidens' warning to Siegfried that the possession of the ring will bring him to ruin—that only in the water is the gold fruitful of anything but destruction.

The introduction of Siegfried at this juncture, however, calls up more than that particular situation. In the first place, it is impossible not to be aware of the parallel symbolism between the Norse and the Romance legends (the more so since the author of " The Ring " was also the author of " Parsifal ") ; in the second, it introduces the *motif* of fire, though fire in another aspect—the fire of deceit through which the hero must break to awaken Brünehilde.

The Thames Daughters speak in turn. The first :

> " ' Trams and dusty trees.
> Highbury bore me. Richmond and Kew
> Undid me. By Richmond I raised my knees
> Supine on the floor of a narrow canoe.' "

The second :

    " ' My feet are at Moorgate, and my heart
      Under my feet. After the event
      He wept. He promised ' a new start.'
      I made no comment. What should I resent ? ' "

The third :

    " ' On Margate Sands.
      I can connect
      Nothing with nothing.
      The broken fingernails of dirty hands.
      My people humble people who expect
      Nothing.' "

In the song of the first there are two references, one to the beginning of the section, with its nymphs of summer nights, the other to Dante's "Purgatorio," where a spirit, saved from Hell at the last moment, greets the poet : "Remember me, who am La Pia. Siena made me, Maremma unmade me : this is known to him who after due engagement wedded me with this ring."

As the river flows on, the tone becomes more hopeless ; in the City daughter it is not perhaps fanciful to glimpse the typist again ; then, finally, in the grim thumbnail sketch of the sands of Margate, swept by the open sea, the matter is concluded. Here are " the crowds of people," the futility, the squalor, the butchering of life to make a proletarian holiday—" the broken finger-nails of dirty hands. My people humble people who expect nothing." It is a vision of a waste land in six short lines.

Then at last sounds the call to repentance, to renunciation :

" To Carthage then I came

Burning burning burning burning
O Lord Thou pluckest me out
O Lord Thou pluckest

burning."

But Carthage is a new Carthage. It is St. Augustine speaking in his " Confessions " ; " To Carthage then I came, where a cauldron of unholy loves sang all about mine ears." With this great representative document of Western asceticism is placed its fellow from the East, the Fire Sermon whose import is implicit in the repetition of the single word " burning." On

this note, having evoked background and beliefs
so vast that they are a literature in themselves,
the section ends.

§ 6. IV—*Death by Water*

The symbolism of this short episode must be,
by now, sufficiently apparent. It consists of
eight lines only :

" Phlebas the Phœnician, a fortnight dead,
　Forgot the cry of gulls, and the deep sea swell
　And the profit and loss.
　　　　　　　　　A current under sea
　Picked his bones in whispers.　As he rose and fell
　He passed the stages of his age and youth
　Entering the whirlpool.
　　　　　　　　　Gentile or Jew
　O you who turn the wheel and look to windward,
　Consider Phlebas, who was once handsome and tall
　　as you."

It is perhaps worth noting the typical Elizabethan
play on words (the merchant being a seller of
currants), such as Shakespeare employs in Lady
Macbeth's "I'll gild the faces of the grooms
withal, For it must seem their guilt." It is
also interesting to compare the whole passage

with Eliot's earlier French version of it in
" Dans le Restaurant,"

" Phlébas, le Phénicien, pendant quinze jours noyé,
    Oubliait les cris des mouettes et la houle de Cor-
      nouaille,
    Et les profits et les pertes, et la cargaison d'étain :
    Un courant de sous-mer l'emporta très loin,
    Le repassant aux étapes de sa vie antérieure.
    Figurez-vous donc, c'était un sort pénible ;
    Cependant, ce fut jadis un bel homme, de haute
      taille."

§ 7. V—*What the Thunder Said*

The fifth and closing section of " The Waste
Land " falls into three divisions. In the first
we at last reach the Chapel Perilous :

        " . . . Then a damp gust
Bringing rain."

In the second we hear the voice of God in the
thunder. In the third, we glance back over the
whole poem.

" In the first part," says the note, " three
themes are employed : the journey to Emmaus,
the approach to the Chapel Perilous and the
present decay of Eastern Europe." It opens

with the passage quoted at the beginning of this
chapter :

" After the torchlight red on sweaty faces
　　After the frosty silence in the gardens
　　After the agony in stony places
　　The shouting and the crying
　　Prison and palace and reverberation
　　Of thunder of spring over distant mountains
　　He who was living is now dead
　　We who were living are now dying
　　With a little patience."

At the centre of it we can still see, as we saw then,
the Crucifixion. But now it is symbolical rather
than historical. The " sweaty faces " belong to
a larger mob than the Jews and Romans who
'' came out with swords and staves to take Him.''
The gardens, bound by frosty silence, are
world-scattered. The agony in a stony place is
more than the triumph of obedience in Gethsemane ; it is the trial of endurance in the Waste
Land. The prison and the palace are not
localised in Jerusalem. Even he who is now
dead is not Jesus alone, but also the Dead Knight
and the slain Vegetation God, Tammuz and

Osiris and Adonis and Orpheus, and the strange mystic character in " the wicked pack of cards," " The Hanged Man " of the Tarots. He is the greatest and eternal renunciation of the flesh by which alone life can come, the stupendous paradox of salvation by loss alone.

This specific identification of Jesus with the gods of the mystery cults is not merely a synthesis elicited from the modern study of comparative religion, but the key to the connection between the Fertility Ritual and the Grail Romance. And although the sect of early Christian Gnostics which emphasised this identification was discountenanced as heretical, their teaching enhances the greatness of the Crucified One. For so the centre of Christian belief becomes also the centre of world belief. Jesus is truly " the Lamb slain from the foundation of the world."

In her chapter devoted to these matters, Miss Weston quotes Mr. G. R. S. Mead's excellent summary : " The claim of these Gnostics was practically that Christianity, or rather the Good

News of the Christ, was precisely the consummation of the inner doctrine of the Mystery-institutions of all the nations." Or, as the famous "Naassene Document" (which is the basis of our knowledge of the sect) has it, " the True Gate is Jesus the Blessed."

Thus the teaching of the cults is seen to culminate in the Crucifixion. Already, in pre-Christian times, the crude " sympathetic " folk-lore had been used as a vehicle for conveying the highest ethical and religious truths : the Attis legend had been so used by the Neo-Platonists ; the Grail legend was to continue the process. " The Exoteric side of the cult," says Miss Weston, " gives us the Human, the Folk-lore elements—the Suffering King ; the Waste Land ; the effect upon the Folk : the task that lies before the hero ; the group of Grail symbols. The Esoteric side provides us with the Mystic Meal, the Food of Life, connected in some mysterious way with a Vessel which is the centre of the combination bearing a well-known ' generative ' significance ; a double initiation into

the source of the lower and higher spheres of
Life : the ultimate proof of the successful issue
of the final test in the restoration of the King."

Restoration is not yet.   It is still the country
of Belladonna, " Lady of the Rocks."

> " Here is no water but only rock,
>   Rock and no water and the sandy road
>   The road winding above among the mountains
>   Which are mountains of rock without water."

This agony of thirst becomes so unendurable
that even the " water-dripping song " of the
hermit-thrush would be a relief :

> " If there were water
> And no rock
> If there were rock
> And also water
> And water
> A spring
> A pool among the rock
> If there were the sound of water only
> Not the cicada
> And dry grass singing
> But sound of water over a rock
> Where the hermit-thrush sings in the pine trees
> Drip drop drip drop drop drop drop,
> But there is no water,"

and fever takes the brain. It is the moment of
mirage.

In an account of one of the Antarctic expedi-
tions, Eliot tells us that he read " that the party
of explorers, at the extremity of their strength,
had the constant delusion that there was *one
more member* than could actually be counted."
This story, combined with the panting vision of
the Resurrected One appearing to the two
disciples on the road to Emmaus, becomes

" Who is the third who walks always beside you ?
When I count, there are only you and I together
But when I look ahead up the white road
There is always another one walking beside you
Gliding wrapt in a brown mantle, hooded
I do not know whether a man or a woman
—But who is that on the other side of you ? "

and with the chaotic inconsequence of a phantas-
magoria, the hooded figure brings to mind the
hooded barbarian hordes mustering on the
drought-cracked plains of a geographically located
waste land, awaiting the overthrow of our
Western culture :

" What is that sound high in the air
Murmur of maternal lamentation,
Who are those hooded hordes swarming
Over endless plains, stumbling in cracked earth
Ringed by the flat horizon only
What is the city over the mountains
Cracks and reforms and bursts in the violet air,
Falling towers,
Jerusalem, Athens, Alexandria,
Vienna, London,
Unreal."

The word " unreal " recalls two earlier glimpses
of London in the first and third sections—the
" unreal city " first " under the brown fog of a
winter dawn," then " under the brown fog of a
winter noon." Now, in the fifth, it is night,
insane with dreams :

" A woman drew her long black hair out tight
And fiddled whisper music on those strings,
And bats with baby faces in the violet light
Whistled, and beat their wings
And crawled head downward down a blackened wall
And upside down in air were towers
Tolling reminiscent bells, that kept the hours
And voices singing out of empty cisterns and
    exhausted wells."

Only the allusive reminiscence of Saint Mary

Woolnoth connects the city with the land round
the Chapel Perilous :

> " In this decayed hole among the mountains
> In the faint moonlight."

At the goal of the Quest all the forces of evil
gather to make one last effort to deter the Knight.
They assail his reason, so that he fears madness.
He is haunted by ghosts and ghouls ; the smell
of death and dread of ultimate and nameless
horror. Worst of all, a hideous suspicion that
the Chapel itself is a delusion :

> " There is the empty chapel, only the wind's home.
> It has no windows, and the door swings,
> Dry bones can harm no one."

But, in the desolation there is the cry of the
herald of dawn :

> " Only a cock stood on the rooftree
> Co co rico co co rico,
> In a flash of lightning."

And the Quest ends :

> " Then a damp gust
> Bringing rain."

The second part of the section which contains

the message of the thunder is retrospective in point of time. The rain is still awaited, for the echo in the mountains is only the " dry sterile thunder without rain." Over the Himalayas the black clouds are gathering, but the Ganges is not at the flood, and the leaves are limp with thirst, while

> " The jungle crouched, humped in silence.
> Then spoke the thunder."

A simple onomatopoetic representation of the noise of thunder is DADADA, and round this is woven an Indian legend of great antiquity. It tells how the sons of the Supreme Lord of Creation (Prajapati) went to dwell as novices with their Father. They were divided into three orders, Gods, Men and Angels (Azuri). When the time of their novitiate was over, the Gods said : " Speak to us, O Lord." The Supreme Lord of Creation uttered the one syllable— " Da," and demanded if they had understood its meaning aright. They answered, "We have understood. You say to us ' DAmyata ' (' Control ! ')." In the same way the Men asked him,

were answered likewise and understood by it
" DAtta " (" Give ! "). And the Angels, ask-
ing and being answered, knew that for them it
was " DAyadhvam " (" Sympathise ! "). This
is the threefold message of the Supreme Lord of
Creation when his voice is heard in the thunder.

First the human duty :

" DA
  Datta : what have we given?
  My friend, blood shaking my heart,
  The awful daring of a moment's surrender
  Which an age of prudence can never retract
  By this, and this only, we have existed
  Which is not to be found in our obituaries
  Or in memories draped by the beneficent spider
  Or under seals broken by the lean solicitor
  In our empty rooms."

The only " difficult " line here—" memories
draped by the beneficent spider "—is explained
by a reference to Webster's " . . . ere the
spider make a thin curtain for your epitaphs."
The general purport of the passage is clear
enough. To exist only by virtue of surrender is
the first condition of man's life. That " awful
daring " is his supreme act. For only by sub-

mitting his will to the greater Will can he live at all. We are back at the Inferno, again, shuddering to see the vast, aimless crowd, scorned by both Heaven and Hell, who are lost because they dared not lose themselves. " He that seeketh his life . . ."

If the human duty of self-giving is sufficiently hard, the angelic duty of sympathetic self-projection would seem, for most men, impossible:

" DA
    Dayadhvam : I have heard the key
    Turn in the door once and turn once only
    We think of the key, each in his prison
    Thinking of the key, each confirms a prison
    Only at nightfall, æthereal rumours
    Revive for a moment a broken Coriolanus."

The inevitable isolation of the individual has burdened the songs of all the poets. Indeed, the theme has been oversung to an extent which makes it suspect of being a stock " poetic " pose. So Eliot, in a note, calls in a philosopher's prose statement to redress the balance. " My external sensations," writes F. H. Bradley in " Appearance and Reality," " are no less private to myself than are my thoughts or my feelings. In either case my experience falls within my own circle, a circle closed on the outside; and, with all its elements alike, every sphere is opaque to the others which surround it. . . . In brief, regarded as an existence which appears in a soul, the whole world for each is peculiar and private to that soul.''

How, then, if the circle is '' closed on the outside '' is sympathy possible? Must we rely solely on those other-worldly '' æthereal rumours '' to revive us in our miserable isolation, leaving the angelic duty to the angels ? It seems so. Yet there is a hint of escape, when we read the '' Dayadhvam '' passage in conjunction with the '' Datta.'' If we have truly surrendered, we shall be less obsessed with self. It is by *thinking of the key* that each confirms his prison.

Finally the divine duty :

'' DA
  Damyata : The boat responded
  Gaily, to the hand expert with sail and oar
  The sea was calm, your heart would have responded
  Gaily, when invited, beating obedient
  To controlling hands.''

K

By self-surrender and by sympathy we gain the right to control others. But on no other terms. And for the majority of us, to ape divinity is dangerous, since we cannot fulfil even the human duty. Control for us must mean only self-control.

The lines convey this truth by very simple means—by using the imagery of the boat and the sea to recall the selfish passion of Tristan and Isolde (in the first section), followed by the implied renunciation of the "would have." At the same time, the reference to the legend itself makes it clear that renunciation is not an end in itself. Control of the means of life is still the highest privilege—when we are fit for it. That, too, is the secret of the Grail.

The close of the poem is a recapitulation of the whole :

> "I sat upon the shore
> Fishing, with the arid plain behind me.
> Shall I at least set my lands in order?
> London Bridge is falling down falling down falling
>   down.
> *Poi s'ascose nel foco che gli affina*

Quando fiam ceu chelidon—O swallow swallow
Le Prince d'Aquitaine à la tour abolie.
These fragments I have shored against my ruins,
Why then Ile fit you. Hieronymo's mad againe.
Datta. Dayadhvam. Damyata.
        Shantih shantih shantih."

The last line of Cante XXVI. of Dante's
" Purgatorio "—" *Poi s'ascose nel foco che gli
affina* " (" Then he dived back into that fire
which refines them ")—is pregnant with associations. Historically, in introducing Arnaut
Daniel, greatest of the Troubadours, friend of
Richard Cœur de Lion, it evokes that magnificent Provençal civilisation and the singers
who bequeathed the Romance legends to the
modern world. Symbolically it gives, at last,
a Christian interpretation to the element of fire,
and at the same time epitomises the poem by
reminding us of the penitential suffering of the
Lustful. Poetically, it recalls those Provençal
verses which recur so often in Eliot's work :

> " Ara vos prec, per aquella valor
> que vos guida al som de l'escalina,
> sovegna vos a temps de ma dolor."

(" And so I pray you, by that Virtue which leads you to the summit of the stairway, remember, in due time, my pain.")

The next quotation is from the " Pervigilium Veneris," the strange, exquisite " The Eve of St. Venus " which is the link between classical and mediæval literature, " the earliest known poem belonging in spirit to the literature of the Middle Ages." Its continual refrain " To-morrow shall be love for the loveless and for the lover to-morrow shall be love," the atmosphere of mysterious excitement which preludes the re-awakening of life, make it of all spring songs the loveliest. Walter Pater, in his reconstruction of the manner of its writing, has described it as " a kind of nuptial hymn, which, taking its start from the thought of nature as the universal mother, celebrated the preliminary pairing and mating together of all fresh things, in the hot and genial springtime—the immemorial nuptials of the soul of the spring itself and the brown earth." And, though its authorship is unknown, for most of us it can have been written only as Pater has described it in "Marius the Epicurean"

—by the dying Flavian " tremulously dictating one stanza more " as the haunting refrain

" Cras amet qui nunquam amavit,
  Quique amavit cras amet,"

comes floating through the window from the throats of the strong young men.

Eliot's use of it by quotation refers us again to the myth of the nightingale, though this time not to Philomela herself, but to her sister, Procne—" Quam fiam ceu chelidon "—"When shall I be as the swallow ? " The complete stanza runs : " The maid of Tereus sings under the shade of the poplar, so that you would think tunes of love came trilling from her mouth and not a sister's complaint of a barbarous lord. She sings, we are dumb. When is my spring coming ? What shall I be as the swallow, that I may cease to be voiceless? " " O swallow, swallow "— bird of spring, and also, in Christian tradition, the bird of consolation which hovered over the Cross crying " Console ! Console ! " "When is my spring coming ? "

But the line from Gérard de Nerval's sonnet " El Desdichado " denies consolation :

" Je suis le ténébreux—le veuf—l'inconsolé,
   Le prince d'Aquitaine à la tour abolie :
   Ma seule étoile est morte—et mon luth constellé
   Porte le soleil noir de la mélancolie."

Here, by association, we are again among the Troubadours (Gérard de Nerval's sonnet was suggested by " The Disinherited Knight " of Scott's " Ivanhoe," and the appellation " prince d'Aquitaine " is primarily associated in most minds with Cœur de Lion) ; we are at the Dark Tower in the Waste Land not far from the Chapel Perilous ; we are gazing at the most sinister card in the Tarot pack, " The Tower struck by Lightning."

The madness of Hieronymo revenging his murdered son in Kyd's " Spanish Tragedy " recalls the hallucinatory episodes of the poem which themselves are concentrated round the entrance to the Chapel Perilous. Then, after the threefold message of the thunder, is the threefold benediction—" Shantih shantih shantih," the formal ending to an Upanishad, of which " The Peace which passeth understanding " is but a feeble translation.

VII

"The Word within a Word"

ELIOT has described his general point of view as "anglo-catholic in religion," adding that the term does not rest with him to define. His early upbringing and environment were puritan, and for him now the antithesis to "Catholic" is "agnostic." These three clues to his position are supplemented by continual references in his prose and poetry.

If it is difficult for a romantic age to appreciate a classicist, for a rebellious age to sympathise with a traditionalist, for a journalistic age to care for literature, it is almost impossible for an irreligious age to understand a man so intensely religious as Eliot. I use the word in a strict sense ; by religion I do not mean a vague code of " playing the game " or a vaguer hope in the " ultimate decency of things " ; I mean belief

in a dogma, which is so wide that it embraces
the whole of life and so narrow that it excludes
as heretics the majority of modern thinkers ;
a creed like a challenge, dividing those who
believe the doctrine of the Incarnation from
those who do not. Incarnation is the vital
issue. Thus Eliot makes one of the Wise
Men speak :

> " . . . were we led all that way for
> Birth or Death? There was a Birth, certainly,
> We had evidence and no doubt. I had seen birth
>   and death,
> But had thought they were different ; this Birth
>   was
> Hard and bitter agony for us, like Death, our death
> We returned to our places, these Kingdoms,
> But no longer at ease here, in the old dispensation,
> With an alien people clutching their gods."

To-day, however, it is not only certain Magi
who are troubled by the doctrine. It is the
Unwise Men who presume to doubt where they
have never thought. "The majority of man-
kind," as Eliot says, "is lazy-minded, incurious,
absorbed in vanities and tepid in emotion, and
is therefore incapable of either much doubt or

much faith ; and when the ordinary man calls himself a sceptic or an unbeliever, that is ordinarily a simple pose, cloaking a disinclination to think anything out to a conclusion.'' Such men, whether professing religion or scepticism, will hardly care to understand Eliot's spiritual pilgrimage from puritanism to anglo-catholicism. It is not an episode in the vulgar brawl of Church v. Chapel, or a spectacular journey from the City Temple to All Saints', Margaret Street. It is simply that Eliot thought out to a conclusion the puritanism which was his inheritance, and discovered that the conclusion was catholicism.

To use a figure. Creeds must not be visualised as paths leading in different directions, so that to take one means to refuse the other, but as circles ever widening from one centre so that each new phase of experience incorporates the last. Eliot has not denied his puritanism ; he has enlarged it. He has not abandoned its self-reliant individualism, its stern self-discipline, its fidelity to vision ; but he has seen that these virtues, when given their true proportion by opposition with their complements, shine the brighter. A scheme of salvation—or, if you prefer it, a rule of life—must prescribe for the many as well as for the one ; self-discipline is valuable only when *directed* to an unselfish end ; and unflinching witness to a vision is no guarantee that the vision is not narrow and limited. There must be place for the priest as well as for the prophet ; for the conserver of the form as well as for the innovator.

The acknowledgment of the importance of form ("the spirit killeth but the letter giveth life"), and the reverence for tradition, which distinguish Eliot's entire outlook, made his conversion inevitable. It was intolerable to be cut off from the main stream ; it was impossible to regard a small tributary as the great river. There was Milton ; but what was Milton beside Dante ? And what, even beside Milton, the New England heritage where

"Upon the glazen shelves kept watch
Matthew and Waldo, guardians of the faith,
The army of unalterable law" ?

But, at the same time, the tradition he followed was an English tradition. For an Englishman with his approach there was no other way. In his essay on Lancelot Andrewes he writes : "The English Church has no literary monument equal to that of Dante, no intellectual monument equal to that of St. Thomas, no devotional monument equal to that of St. John of the Cross, no building so beautiful as the Cathedral of Modena or the basilica of St. Zeno in Verona. But there are those for whom the City churches are as precious as any of the four hundred odd churches in Rome which are in no danger of demolition, and for whom St. Paul's, in comparison with St. Peter's, is not lacking in decency ; and the English devotional verse of the seventeenth century—admitting the one difficult case of conversion, that of Crashaw—finer than that of any other country or religion at the time. The intellectual achievement and the prose style of Hooker and Andrewes came to complete the structure of the English Church as the philosophy of the thirteenth century crowns the Catholic Church."

Eliot has given assent to a creed which can claim Dante as well as Donne, the "Summa" as well as the "Ecclesiastical Polity," which understands and incorporates the heritage of post-Reformation England as well as pre-Reformation Europe. The crux of it is this—that a Celebration in the simplest country church in England to-day perpetuates a form which itself is an epitome of civilisation. Into it are woven the fear and wonder and cruelty and joy which was primitive religion ; the austerity of Greece and the magnificence of Rome, the turbulent colour of the Middle Ages and the daring thought of the Renaissance ; the rhythm of the body's movement and the power of words, the delight of eye and ear. And this form, itself a thing of sufficient wonder, is used to embody a truth, an esoteric doctrine, which is the clue to the riddle of existence—the doctrine of the Incarnation.

Incarnation is no more a specifically Christian doctrine than is the idea of the Slain and Resurrected god ; in both cases Christianity has adapted and fulfilled earlier manifestations. But in any form the doctrine is supremely important. In one of her books Mary Butts points out that a symptom of an age's decadence is the repudiation of this idea of a God-Man in favour of a Man-God, the substitution of Deification for Incarnation. Though the obvious example is the end of Imperial Rome, the process is hardly less noticeable in contemporary life, where deification has become an almost daily occurrence and the whole trend of thought is toward Man's triumph and away from God's salvation.

Eliot, as puritan, was no less affected by the doctrine than he is as catholic, for it is common to all Christian communities. Yet it is true to say that the catholic *stresses* it more than the puritan. There is, indeed, in religious thought a perpetually shifting emphasis on the Incarnation and the Atonement. Though the two dogmas are, of course, inseparable, in an age when one is dominant, the other suffers a corresponding diminution. Individualistic puritanism naturally tends to emphasise the Death at the expense of the Birth, to see the Crucifixion largely in terms of the Divine rebel killed by an unworthy society. The danger here is the shortness of the step from the idea of a Slain God to the idea of a Slain Man ; then immediately we are in the world of Hero-cults and Deification. It is no accident that " modern " protestant thought insists less and less on the Divinity of Jesus but concentrates on His teaching and His death. Yet it is the Incarnation alone that gives meaning to the Crucifixion, makes it anything more than a martyrdom. It was God, become Man, who was killed ; not Man who, being killed, became God.

Once the Incarnation is acknowledged, there is no *reason* against embracing the whole of catholic dogma. Admit the amazing incon-sequence of the miracle that at a particular time in the world's history God should become incarnate as a Jewish carpenter, and you cannot logically refuse to admit any other miracle arising from it—the miracle, for instance, of the meta-morphosis of bread and wine into the Divine

Body and Blood. Protestantism is a half-way house where one takes refuge because of that "disinclination to think the matter out to a conclusion." Only the catholic and the agnostic dare to reach the end of their journeys.

The protestant, however, can accompany Eliot at least some of the way. He does not deny the central doctrine; he only disputes certain of its implications. The agnostic can never comprehend the poet at all. And the criticism of his poems by agnostics has been no less unjust to their content than the examination by romantics to their form. The fact that Eliot sees the futility and misery of life does not mean that he acquiesces in it, much less that he regards it as final. Because he accepts the Church's doctrine, he is not blind to her faults, and the very bitterness of his early satire is a measure of his belief. But for the atheist the futility is all—an evidence of the absence of a Guide, while the incompetence and failure of the Church are sufficient to invalidate her teaching. The atheist questions and doubts; the Christian questions but believes. To the sceptic, faith is an evasion : to the believer, an answer. And the one cannot understand the other.

" Every man who thinks and lives by thought," says Eliot, " must have his own scepticism, that which stops at the question, that which ends in denial, or that which leads to faith and which is somehow integrated into the faith which transcends it." This transcendance, true of the intellect where " the demon of doubt is inseparable from the spirit of belief," is true on other planes too. Eliot is one of " those who doubt, but who have the mind to conceive, and the sensibility to feel, the disorder, the futility, the meaninglessness, the mystery of life and suffering, and who can only find peace through a satisfaction of the whole being." Such satisfaction—satisfaction for the poet, for the traditionalist, for the thinker, for the scholar, and for the struggling human being in him—he finds in catholic Christianity. No lesser thing will do. And as the conviction of it deepens, it is reflected more and more in his poetry.

Eliot's individualistic approach to catholicism, his innate puritanism and his intense devoutness have combined to make him the author of the most scathing satire on the Church in modern poetry. He is too angry even for the deadly urbanity of Siegfried Sassoon's comment on the days

" when first the Dean went pious,
—For possible preferment sacrificed
His hedonistic and patrician bias,
And offered his complacency to Christ."

He is concerned, too, not with individuals, but with the institution itself.

" The hippo's feeble steps may err
In compassing material ends,
While the True Church need never stir
To gather in its dividends."

And the indictment proceeds in ever more violent imagery, till we see the apotheosis of the hippopotamus :

" He shall be washed as white as snow,
By all the martyr'd virgins kist,
While the True Church remains below
Wrapt in the old miasmal mist."

This poem, for its savage intensity, is unique, but
L

in " Mr. Eliot's Sunday Morning Service," there is an ironic disquiet, though this time on a lower plane, when :

> " The sable presbyters approach
> The avenue of penitence ;
> The young are red and pustular
> Clutching piaculative pence "

in the church where :

> " A painter of the Umbrian school
> Designed upon a gesso ground
> The nimbus of the Baptized God.
>
> The wilderness is cracked and browned
> But through the water pale and thin
> Still shine the unoffending feet
> And there above the painter set
> The Father and the Paraclete."

More incongruous still is the company of people making their Easter Communion in " Gerontion," when

> " In the juvescence of the year
> Came Christ the tiger "

with the mystery of His Body and Blood :

> " To be eaten, to be divided, to be drunk
> Among whispers ; by Mr. Silvero
> With caressing hands, at Limoges
> Who walked all night in the next room ;

By Hakagawa, bowing among the Titians ;
By Madame de Tornquist, in the dark room
Shifting the candles ; Fraulein von Kulp
Who turned in the hall, one hand on the door."

This poem, too, is remarkable as marking a further stage of Eliot's religious pilgrimage. The early individual emotion of the " Preludes " :

" His soul stretched tight across the skies
    That fade behind a city block,
    Or trampled by insistent feet
    At four and five and six o'clock ;

    And short square fingers stuffing pipes
  . And evening newspapers, and eyes
    Assured of certain certainties,
    The conscience of a blackened street
    Impatient to assume the world.

    I am moved by fancies that are curled
    Around these images, and cling :
    The notion of some infinitely gentle
    Infinitely suffering thing."

has widened and deepened, has been fused with profounder thought, and finds expression in the great passage :

" After such knowledge, what forgiveness ? Think
        now
    History has many cunning passages, contrived
        corridors

And issues, deceives with whispering ambitions,
Guides us by vanities. Think now
She gives when our attention is distracted
And what she gives, gives with such supple con-
      fusions
That the giving famishes the craving. Gives too
      late
What's not believed in, or if still believed,
In memory only, reconsidered passion. Gives too
      soon
Into weak hands, what's thought can be dispensed
      with
Till the refusal propagates a fear. Think
Neither fear nor courage saves us. Unnatural vices
Are fathered by our heroism. Virtues
Are forced upon us by our impudent crimes.
These tears are shaken from the wrath-bearing
      tree."

Nor are we far, at least in spirit, from " Ash Wednesday," when the disquiet inspired by the eyes " assured of certain certainties " becomes the exclamation of relief in renouncement :

" Because I do not hope to know again
The infirm glory of the positive hour."

It might be said without injustice that none of Eliot's poetry is conspicuous for that " infirm glory." His " positive hour " seems to have

ended before he started to write. From the
beginning he has questioned ironically, noted
incongruities, stated cynical contrasts. But this
need not imply scepticism ; merely sensitiveness.
We may protest that we have never seen the
world so, that we are untroubled by these
observations ; but such an admission condemns
not Eliot's vision but our lack of it. It con-
victs us of that facile optimism which refuses to
face unpalatable facts, that fear which makes
ostriches of us all. Only the reader who is both
sensitive and brave can look at what the poet
sees. Then, in the splendour of morning, he,
too, will be :

> " aware of the damp souls of housemaids
>   Sprouting despondently at area gates,"

though his interpretation of the fact will depend
on his convictions. The sensitive agnostic may
see only the absence of God, where the sensitive
Christian sees the sin of man.

This difference in outlook can be further
illustrated by the Sweeney poems, when the
brutal indifference of Sweeney to the epileptic

demi-mondaine is compared with the desertion of Ariadne by Theseus or when the whispered plot to murder Sweeney recalls the killing of the great Agamemnon. In both cases ancient heroes are brought down to the level of the modern vulgarian. This, to a hero-worshipping age, is intolerable. Here, cries the agnostic, is cynicism *in excelsis*. Here, retorts the Christian, is a necessary iconoclasm. For if Agamemnon is Sweeney, Sweeney is also Agamemnon ; you must have it both ways. And the point is surely that there is no difference in *kind* between the highest and the lowest of men ; there is difference only in *degree*. The finest hero and the hollowest villain have something in common. But the gulf between the finest hero and God is infinite.

Again we are back at the fundamental issue of Incarnation or Deification. The one involves the destruction of the other, and the destructiveness of Eliot's earlier phase can only be understood aright in the light of the later credos. What to the agnostic is a reprehensible degradation is to the Christian the preparation of the pathway to

Humility, the cardinal virtue from which all the others spring and without which they are of none effect.

After "The Waste Land" and "The Hollow Men" come the two short poems on the Incarnation, "Journey of the Magi" (from which quotation has been made at the beginning of this chapter) and "A Song for Simeon" with its Prayer of the Threshold :

> "Let the Infant, the still unspeaking and unspoken Word,
> Grant Israel's consolation
> To one who has eighty years and no to-morrow.
>
> According to Thy word,
> They shall praise Thee and suffer in every genera-
> tion
> With glory and derision,
> Light upon light, mounting the saints' stair.
> Not for me the martyrdom, the ecstasy of thought
> and prayer,
> Not for me the ultimate vision.
> Grant me Thy peace."

These two poems prepared readers for "Ash Wednesday." Until they appeared, it was possible to mistake Eliot's direction. The mood of despair in " The Hollow Men " might have resulted in denial instead of faith. " The Waste Land " might have meant defeat. And even now it is not sufficiently realised that, for an Eliot, " Ash Wednesday " is the inevitable sequel to " The Waste Land." There is still a tendency to regard him as a modern poet who expressed his age—an age of disgust and despair— in one magnificent poem and then flew off at a tangent to indulge in slight religious verse of a mediæval flavour.

" Ash Wednesday " is thus often under-rated, and under-rated, be it noted, on the grounds of the *belief* it involves. Agnostic readers, whether private or professional critics, were and are annoyed because the poet who, in " The Waste Land," provided them with an expression of their own hopelessness should, in " Ash Wednesday," turn on them with an implied condemnation of it. They fail to see that Eliot is quite consistent, considering only that to them the transition would be inconsistent. And because they feel strongly about the matter,

they are unwilling in approaching the poem to
" suspend both belief and disbelief."   " There
is a difference," writes Eliot in his essay on
" Dante," " between philosophical *belief* and
poetic *assent*. . . . You are not called upon to
believe what Dante believed, for your belief will
not give you a groat's worth more of understanding and appreciation : but you are called
upon more and more to understand it. . . . I
will not deny that it may be in practice easier for
a Catholic to grasp the meaning in many places,
than for the ordinary agnostic ; but that is not
because the Catholic believes, but because he has
been instructed. It is a matter of knowledge and
ignorance, not of belief and scepticism."

If this is true of Dante's poetry, it is equally
true of Eliot's. The difficulty is that, when
religious convictions are involved, the requisite
detachment is so unconscionably difficult. Dante
is decently dead, so that literary appreciation of
him is *de rigueur* for many people whom he would
have unhesitatingly relegated to the Inferno.
Eliot is challengingly alive, and his opponents

do not hesitate to seek to discredit his beliefs by denigrating his poetic expression of them.

I should not presume, in view of Eliot's theory of poetry, to consider " Ash Wednesday " a personal confession were it not that he himself, by his avowal of his religious tenets, has provided some justification. Yet the personal element must not be unduly stressed. The " man who suffers " is still, to a certain extent, separate from the " mind which creates." · To return to the " Dante," " we can make a distinction between what Dante believes as a poet and what he believed as a man," and we must remember that " a coherent traditional system of dogma and morals like the Catholic . . . stands apart, for understanding and assent even without belief, from the single individual who propounds it." But it is still true to say on the one hand that criticism of " Ash Wednesday " is, consciously or unconsciously, influenced by the reader's attitude to Catholicism and, on the other, that appreciation depends largely on a sympathy with Eliot's personal position.

On the literary side, it may be conceded that in parts it shows a certain lessening of intensity. The simplicity is not always the refined essence of the thing ; the imagery is occasionally trite ; experiments are sometimes unsuccessful ; the echo sounds not always sufficiently resonant. For instance, the lines :

" No place of grace for those who avoid the face
    No time to rejoice for those who walk among noise
        and deny the voice "

seem to me to defeat their own object by inevitably attracting too much attention to the oral structure, whereas the earlier :

" Came Christ the tiger
    In depraved May,"

with its brilliant onomatopoetic use of the long, languorous " a," contrasted with the short, active " i," is altogether successful because it is so unobtrusive.

Or again, the Swinburnian echo of :

" And the last heart stiffens and rejoices
    In the lost lilac and the lost sea voices
    And the weak spirit quickens to rebel
    For the bent golden-rod and the lost sea-smell "

is too obvious from a poet who has given us the mermaid picture :

" I have seen them riding seaward on the waves
    Combing the white hair of the waves blown back
    When the wind blows the water white and black."

Nor does

" Going in white and blue, in Mary's colour,"

by limiting the image, manage to divorce itself in the mind from the crudely coloured statues of Our Lady to be found in Continental churches and Catholic Repositories—an association which, in the context, destroys its effectiveness.

These are, I think, legitimate criticisms. What is not legitimate is to compare " Ash Wednesday " with " The Waste Land " in its scope or with the earlier poems in its intention. It is utterly different from both. " Ash Wednesday " is a Bach prelude ; " The Waste Land " a Beethoven symphony. The early poems are Hogarth ; " Ash Wednesday," Giotto. It must be judged for what it is, not blamed for not being something else. And even its faults become apparent only when compared with Eliot's own earlier work.

The continuity of "Ash Wednesday" from "The Waste Land" may be easily seen by noticing a similarity of thought in each poem. It will be remembered that the message of the thunder inspires the lines :

> "The awful daring of a moment's surrender
> Which an age of prudence can never retract
> By this, and this only, have we existed"

—that surrender becoming the highest human duty, the first step toward salvation. In the fifth poem of "Ash Wednesday" we have the prayer for those who :

> "are terrified and cannot surrender
> And affirm before the world and deny between the rocks,"

while in the first we find that the poet has himself made his own surrender. Not only

> "Because I do not hope to know again
> The infirm glory of the positive hour,"

but

> "Because these wings are no longer wings to fly
> But merely vans to beat the air
> The air which is now thoroughly small and dry

Smaller and dryer than the will
Teach us to care and not to care
Teach us to sit still."

This is the key in which the whole sequence of six poems is set. At last the personal will has been submitted to the higher, universal Will and renouncement has brought relief. There has come a quietness, a mysterious calm which is, however, more powerful than the passionate tumult which preceded it. All that that potency means only the mystic can understand, but Eliot has given us a hint of it.

The symbolism of bones in the earlier poems is sufficiently clear :

" A twisted branch upon the beach
Eaten smooth, and polished
As if the world gave up
The secret of its skeleton,
Stiff and white."

and

" He knew the anguish of the marrow
The ague of the skeleton ;
No contact possible to flesh
Allayed the fever of the bone "

and

> "Bones cast in a little low dry garret
> Rattled by the rat's foot only, year to year."

But now in the second poem of "Ash Wednesday" this horror, this final dissolution, becomes :

> "Under a juniper-tree, the bones sang, scattered and
> shining
> We are glad to be scattered, we did little good to
> each other,
> Under a tree in the cool of the day, with the
> blessing of sand,
> Forgetting themselves and each other, united
> In the quiet of the desert. This is the land which
> ye
> Shall divide by lot. And neither division nor unity
> Matters. This is the land. We have our inherit-
> ance."

Somehow the triumph of death is no longer a triumph.

The third poem (which, when published separately, was entitled "Som de l'Escalina," recalling the Arnaut Daniel episode in the "Purgatorio") is a record of the pilgrimage, sufficiently important to quote in full :

" At the first turning of the second stair
I turned and saw below
The same shape twisted on the banister
Under the vapour in the fetid air
Struggling with the devil of the stairs who wears
The deceitful face of hope and of despair.

At the second turning of the second stair
I left them twisting, turning below ;
There were no more faces and the stair was dark,
Damp, jaggèd, like an old man's mouth drivelling,
     beyond repair,
Or the toothed gullet of an agèd shark.

At the first turning of the third stair
Was a slotted window bellied like the fig's fruit
And beyond the hawthorn blossom and a pasture
     scene
The broadbacked figure drest in blue and green
Enchanted the maytime with an antique flute.
Blown hair is sweet, brown hair over the mouth
     blown,
Lilac and brown hair ;
Distraction, music of the flute, stops and steps of
     the mind over the third stair,
Fading, fading ; strength beyond hope and despair
Climbing the third stair.

Lord, I am not worthy
Lord, I am not worthy
          but speak the word only."

Here are present the main elements of the sequence—its formalism ; its imagery, at once more obvious and more ambiguous than that of earlier poems ; its background of religious associations ; its atmosphere of struggle. For, as the last poem reminds us, we are :

" Wavering between the profit and the loss
    In this brief transit where the dreams cross
    The dreamcrossed twilight between birth and
        death."

If there is nightmare in " The Waste Land," in " Ash Wednesday " is the dream on the point of waking, that fraction of a second when the phantoms of sleep struggle with the realities of the room. For though the will is surrendered, the full revelation is not yet and " Ash Wednesday " closes with the prayer :

" Blessèd sister, holy mother, spirit of the fountain,
        spirit of the garden,
    Suffer us not to mock ourselves with falsehood
    Teach us to care and not to care
    Teach us to sit still
    Even among these rocks,
    Our peace in His will
    And even among these rocks
    Sister, mother

M

And spirit of the river, spirit of the sea,
Suffer me not to be separated
And let my cry come unto Thee."

The rocks are still there, though it is no longer
Belladonna who sits among them.

The background of " Ash Wednesday," with
its three white leopards and jewelled unicorns,
with the Valley of the bones, the Rose and the
Garden and the yew-trees, with the veiled sister
and the Lady in a white gown and One

" . . . wearing
White light folded, sheathed about her, folded,"

is ritualistic. In " Marina," which followed
" Ash Wednesday," the same vision is expressed
in more general symbolism and with greater
personal intensity. Marina, the daughter of
Pericles, who was lost and found again, is the
symbol of the old vision transcended. The poem
is as full of the sea as " The Waste Land " was of
drought. The ship which the traveller made :

" The rigging weak and the canvas rotten
Between one June and another September.
Made this unknowing, half conscious, unknown,
my own."

is to be abandoned for " the new ships." The
" grace " of the new vision has reduced the old
world with its death-values to something " insub-
stantial." The shores are in sight, the same, yet
profoundly changed as the poet welcomes :

> " What seas what shores what granite islands towards
>   my timbers
> And woodthrush calling through the fog
> My daughter."

In the joy of the new discovery, he does not
forget what he has escaped. Those things he
has made, the children of his mind, might have
been dead. So the epigraph to " Marina " is
a line from Seneca's " Hercules," recalling the
awful moment when the hero, having slain his
children in a fit of madness, recovers his wits and
sees what he has done. Of all the epigraphs—
and all of them, like the titles, are important for
their bearing on the poems they preface—this is
the most dramatic, the most skilfully chosen.
And we share the poet's gratitude that he is not
Hercules but Pericles.

VIII

And Now

THE relation of "Marina" to the poems after "The Waste Land" resembles that of "Gerontion" to those before it. Each of these, the two finest of Eliot's short poems, marks a stage of development both in the outward expression and in the inner vision. Each crystallises what is characteristic of the preceding period, while suggesting what is to follow. As "Gerontion" pointed the way to the masterpiece of 1922, so "Marina" gives promise of the new masterpiece which 1932 sees in the making. It is not yet completed; even its title and plan are, I believe, tentative and subject to modification. Thus it is impossible to assess and dangerous to criticise even the part of it which is published, though certain deductions are possible.

At the moment (July, 1932), the first two
sections of this projected work (which is to be
slightly longer than " The Waste Land ") are
in print—" Triumphal March," in the Ariel
Poems, and " Difficulties of a Statesman,"
which appeared in " Commerce " (Hiver, 1932).
The titles themselves suggest that, as " The
Waste Land " was the post-War world, so
here is the post-Peace world. The poems show
that the problem is still one of adjustment,
though viewed from a different angle. The
interest centres rather on the matter of govern-
ment than on the individual reactions to chaos.
The protagonist of the new poem is the leader of
men :

> " There he is now, look ;
> There is no interrogation in those eyes
> Or in the hands, quiet over the horse's neck,
> And the eyes watchful, waiting, perceiving,
>   indifferent,"

as he appears to the waiting crowds in
" Triumphal March," and the tired man in
" Difficulties of a Statesman " yearning for

" A still moment, repose of noon, set under the
    upper branches of noon's widest tree
Under the breast feather stirred by the small wind
    after noon
There the cyclamen spreads its wings, there the
    clematis droops over the lintel
O mother (not one of these busts all correctly
    inscribed)
I a tired head among these heads
Necks strong to bear them
Noses strong to break the wind
Mother
May we not be some time, almost now, together,
If the mactations, immolations, oblations, impe-
    trations
Are now observed
May we not be
O hidden
Hidden in the stillness of noon, in the silent
    croaking night."

The background of this second part, as well
as a definite reference to the Volscians, suggests
the figure of Coriolanus as the arch-type of
leadership. It thus becomes not altogether
fanciful to refer back to the closing section of
" The Waste Land " and the message of the
thunder. " Give," the human duty of self-
surrender, has been elaborated in " Ash Wednes-

day." and the reward of it glimpsed in
" Marina." But there are also the com-
mands " Sympathise " and " Control " (it
will be remembered in the " Sympathise "
passage occur the lines

" Only at nightfall æthereal rumours
    Revive for a moment a broken Coriolanus ");

and it seems that the new poem is to be devoted
to a similar elaboration of these complementary
themes.

As in " The Waste Land," there is a world-
conspectus and a simultaneity of action. The
triumphal march is not only the Great War
(ironically compressed into a catalogue of fighting
weapons), but all processions which the mob
wildly and foolishly acclaims—the outer show
either masking hollowness or concealing truth.
There is the Roman Triumph and the Boy
Scouts, the " société gymnastique de Poissy "
and the Lord Mayor's Show, the Vestalia and
the Mass. And in " Difficulties of a Statesman "
there are the conferences and committees and

bureaucratic squabblings and interferences which, at all times, surround the reality of power.

The transitions from one age to another, from one plane to another, are, however, considerably compressed and simplified. Eliot now not only takes his own method for granted, but assumes that his readers also will. The juxtaposition of ancient and modern is neither merely contrast, as in the early work, nor hints at identity, as in " The Waste Land," but a compound of both, an assertion of co-existence. This was apparent in " Marina," but it is used more extensively in the new poems, as, for instance,

" Arthur Edward Cyril Parker is appointed telephone
    operator
  At a salary of one pound ten a week rising by
    annual increments of five shillings
  To two pounds ten a week ; with a bonus of thirty
    shillings at Christmas
  And one week's leave a year.
  A committee has been appointed to nominate a
    commission of engineers
  To consider the Water Supply.
  A commission is appointed
  For Public Works, primarily the question of re-
    building the fortifications.

A commission is appointed
To confer with a Volscian commission
About perpetual peace : the fletchers and javelin-
    makers and smiths
Have appointed a joint committee to protest
    against the reduction of orders."

This simplification leads one to hope that, when
the entire poem appears, it will be far more
widely read and appreciated than was its prede-
cessor. In part, of course, Eliot's steadily
increasing reputation will ensure that. But partly,
too, the change will be due to the fact that the
Plain Reader, being familiar with the idiom, will
be able to devote undivided attention to the
content and to surrender to the beauty of the
poetry. Then it will be found, I dare to
prophesy, that T. S. Eliot will be recognised
generally as one of the very few great writers of
the post-War world. As he is.

THE END

INDEX TO POEMS